Praise for *Why Does the Screenwriter*

"*Why Does the Screenwriter Cross the Road?* i
ass. It takes an unusual long-range approach ᴛᴏ sᴄʀᴇᴇɴᴡʀɪᴛɪɴɢ ᴛʜᴀᴛ ɪs
irresistible."
—Charlie Rubin, writer: *Law & Order: Criminal Intent, Seinfeld, In Living Color*;
   professor: NYU Department of Dramatic Writing

"*Why Does the Screenwriter Cross the Road?* is the most complete and
honest book about the process of screenwriting I've ever read. It will
inspire you, guide you, and galvanize you to write the screenplay you've
always wanted to write."
—Michael Pressman, Emmy-winning director and showrunner: *Chicago Hope,
   Picket Fences, Blue Bloods, Justified, Law & Order*

"If you are writing, thinking about writing, or rewriting a script, buy this
wonderful book. It will help you write your best movie."
   —Jacquelyn Reingold, writer/producer: *In Treatment, Smash, Grace & Frankie*

"A unique, insightful guide not only to writing a screenplay, but to your
own creative process as well!"
   — Chad Gervich, writer/producer: *After Lately, Cupcake Wars, Dog With a Blog,
   Wipeout*; author: *How To Manage Your Agent; Small Screen, Big Picture*

"It is brilliantly organized, splendidly written, and essential to read. This
book is written with the savvy that accrues from years of writing and
teaching experience and with the compassion and generosity that comes
from remembering how it was to have only hopes and dreams."
—Hal Ackerman, author: *Write Screenplays That Sell: The Ackerman Way*;
   UCLA screenwriting professor and department chair

"This book is like having a pal along on the journey, a pal who can offer
lots of great practical advice while helping you avoid the traps and pitfalls. Joe Gilford possesses an uncanny ability to condense the complex-
ities of dramatic writing into simple truths."
—John Tintori, award-nominated director and film editor; professor, NYU
   graduate film department

"In a world overflowing with screenwriting books, Gilford opens up new doors to both experienced and new screenwriters. He will make you smarter when it comes to crafting your screenplays."
—DB Gilles, author: *Writers Rehab: A 12-Step for Screenwriters . . .* ; screenwriting professor: NYU

"Don't cross the road without this book. Gilford is a talented writer, a great teacher, and a very funny man. The proof is on every page of this highly enjoyable and very practical guide to the art and craft of the screenwriting trade."
—Paul Thompson, screenwriting professor: NYU

"Whether you're a seasoned pro or an anxious beginner, prepare yourself to be entertained and enlightened by one of the best in the biz."
—Tim Albaugh, director: MFA Screenwriting & TV program, Hollins University; UCLA screenwriting professor

"Gilford's book is packed full of insights that will have you reevaluating exactly what writing a screenplay is."
—Tom Farr, editor: tomfarrwriter.blogspot.com

"Joe Gilford takes you on a journey across the road, showing you all the screenwriting sites in the process. It's definitely a journey worth taking."
—Matthew Terry, screenwriter, filmmaker, teacher

"Joe Gilford gives you all the tools you need to create a powerhouse script. Think of this book as a basic recipe for a delicious screenplay. Each chapter describes an ingredient and why you need to use it. Exercises along the way are where you get to taste what you have created so far. Once you reach the end you will have learned how to serve up a savory story that will leave people wanting more. Grab a copy of this book now and start cookin' on your screenplay!"
—Forris Day Jr., ScaredStiffReviews.com

WHY DOES THE

Screenwriter Cross the Road?

+ OTHER SCREENWRITING SECRETS

JOE GILFORD

MICHAEL WIESE PRODUCTIONS

Published by Michael Wiese Productions
12400 Ventura Blvd. #1111
Studio City, CA 91604
(818) 379-8799, (818) 986-3408 (Fax)
mw@mwp.com
www.mwp.com
Manufactured in the United States
of America

Library of Congress Cataloging-in-Publication Data

Gilford, Joe, 1952–
  Why does the screenwriter cross the road? . . . and
other screenwriting secrets / Joe Gilford.
     pages cm
  ISBN 978-1-61593-223-8
  1. Motion picture authorship. 2. Motion picture
authorship--Vocational guidance. I. Title.
  PN1996.G415 2015
  808.2'3—dc23
                              2014037944

Cover design by Johnny Ink. johnnyink.com
Interior design by Debbie Berne
Copyediting by Gary Sunshine

HOW TO USE THIS BOOK

- If you've been gazing at the same unfinished script for more than one year, then this book will help you start over without throwing everything away. This is an easy way to get back in the saddle.

- If you're a film student — DIVE IN. Although this is a distillation of teaching young filmmakers at NYU since 1999, it is a nonacademic and highly practical guide to getting started, staying with it, and finishing your script, regardless of length.

- If you are a first-time screenwriter, this book is a basic guide to the fundamentals of writing a professional screenplay. Read the whole book and combine it with your overall learning experience.

- If you teach screenwriting, this book will be a good text for second-, third-, and fourth-year undergrads or any level MFA fellows. Use chapters 1 through 6 primarily. However, the entire book contains an insightful overview of practical methods of developing a strong screen story.

- If you've been a screenwriter for some time, you can use this book to refresh your knowledge of why you started doing it in the first place. Rediscover what it is that makes your work unique. Pay special attention to chapters 2 through 6.

- If you are a script analyst, a reader, or a development professional, the entire book can be useful in revealing ideas about screenwriting and storytelling other than simple salability. Here is a different way of understanding the successful screen or television story beyond commercial viability. Pay special attention to chapters 2 through 6.

CONTENTS

Chapter 3
....

SO THERE'S THIS PERSON 78

Chapter 4
....

WHY IS THIS STORY SO IMPORTANT FOR YOUR HERO? ... 89

Chapter 5
....

IF YOU DON'T BELIEVE THIS STORY, WHO WILL? 104

Chapter 6

Chapter 7

Chapter 8

Chapter 9

INTRODUCTION

LET'S ADMIT IT: writing a good screenplay isn't easy. Any seasoned professional, including me, can tell you that.

You really want it to go well. You really want to do a good job. You want those involved — including yourself — to be very pleased.

You really want it to be satisfying for all parties, in this case that means your characters and your audience.

I believe great care is always taken in writing the best screenplays. The story needs to be psychically and spiritually nutritious. This isn't a one-night stand. This is something that needs to be meaningful, maybe even last a lifetime, which is difficult even under the best circumstances.

Believe it or not, in the end, it needs to make sense in some way.

Even if you don't see yourself as some kind of "artist," you can't avoid it. You're going to be writing this script using your whole psyche. All of the feelings, physical sensations, life experiences, sense of human values, and conscious actions you perform are the product of your entire being.

I don't know about you, but the whole idea of my script being good and being liked by people is very personal.

You want this thing to be powerful, memorable, and most of all, you want them coming back for more.

But what feels right? What works? It's different every time you start a new project. What's the next move? What should I do to make this better — and better — and better? How can I make it as satisfying as possible, but at the same time not make it self-conscious or formal?

This is the personal and emotional side of what you do when you write a story.

But there's craft involved.

I like to describe screenwriting as a professional craft, which can be thought of as a combination of music, law, and architecture.

Music: because the creative notation of the written document is absolutely nothing like the beauty of the final product. You don't "see" a screenplay and you don't "listen" to sheet music. But without it, nobody would know how to perform it; how to bring it to life. Ultimately, the reward of a movie and a symphony are actually invisible. The final product is *felt* by its audience.

Law: because, in a story, you've got to prove something to your audience — and it must make sense according to essential human values.

Architecture: because you cannot ignore certain proven principles of cause and effect; because you must have structure so that we understand what it is; because you must respect the rules of engineering so that the whole thing doesn't fall apart.

And for one of the most important reasons you'll learn in this book:

A screenplay is not written — it's built.

This book is intended for anyone who is thinking about writing a script. That could be a feature film, a one-hour drama, a sitcom spec, or a short film, and this includes students, first-time scriptwriters, and professionals who want to revisit the governing principles of our craft or those who just want to take a crack at it.

Orson Welles once said something both funny and cynical: "Anyone can learn anything in this business in forty-five minutes." I actually agree with what sounds like a grotesque undervaluing of the remarkable amount of craft that goes into every aspect of filmmaking.

But what he's right about is that this is like becoming a lumberjack. How much do you actually need to learn that you haven't learned already? And are you ready to listen? And are you ready to cast off so many notions that provide you a toxic kind of comfort for some of your ideas, which may have no business being translated into a screenplay?

The ideas and principles that we'll explore cover the basic principles of all dramatic writing and so it doesn't matter how long or short your script turns out to be.

So let's get something out of the way right at the start. It's just my opinion, but . . .

Film is NOT a visual medium.

Blasphemy?

Okay, if your knees shook or you wanted to punch me in the face maybe this book isn't for you . . . or maybe it is.

If you're an open-minded creative person curious about other points of view and figure "what harm can yet another book on screenwriting do me?" then keep reading.

PROMISE: Read this book, and you'll understand what I'm saying. It will also free you from a lot of ideas and methods that are making it more difficult for you to work through and finish your decent and producible screenplay. It will also help you dispel a lot of delusions about writing scripts that will allow you to use your native talent (which I'm sure you have, otherwise you wouldn't be reading this) and finish a good script that people will read.

This book will help you connect with something that will make your script better than you thought. It's what I call the *human value.* This is what your story is about; what the main character struggles for. It's what audiences really want to see. It's what actors really want to be involved in. But it's not a sermon or an essay. It's a screenplay. A dramatic script that will then go through the amazing process of being transformed into that wonderful final product: a movie.

Remain excited. That's another thing you'll learn to do.

That human value is pretty simple. "Crime doesn't pay." "Love finds a way." "Be yourself." "It's better to be connected to people than not." "Money isn't everything." "Family is important." Yes, just the kind of things everybody struggles for in their everyday lives.

But telling the story of your character struggling with this value needs to be exciting, funny, engaging, and original in some way. Aristotle claimed there was "nothing new under the sun." Yet even with the limited amount of great human values out there, we just can't stop trying to tell those stories in a staggering variety of ways.

Read this book and you'll also have the opportunity to free yourself from the self-judging and inhibiting mindset you bring to your work every day.

It will stop you from hearing certain things from your "savvy" friends, even industry professionals, who pollute your mind with statements like, "Oh, they're only doing horror movies this year" or "Nobody's looking for that."

What this book affirms is that what "they" are looking for is *a good script*. They always have been and they always will be. What this book proposes is to improve the skills that you need in order to write a good screenplay; what I like to call *a screenplay that works*.

Industry professionals, studio executives, even independent producers live in a world of fear. It's not their fault. They come by it honestly. They're frightened of saying "yes" to the wrong thing and just as frightened of saying "no" to the right thing. Best thing you can do is stay out of that dilemma and simply write what you believe works.

Notice I have not used the word *sell*.

Sure, I can tell you which kind of script sells — the one they just bought!

Nobody knows if a script will be produced or if it will sell, so forget about that. And they can't really tell if a movie will be successful. Odds are against every movie being either critically or financially successful anyway. If that's why you picked up this book, just shut it, right now, and go find a book that makes the ultimately false guarantee of helping you write a script that will sell. Won't happen. At least I cannot make that promise. Sorry.

But take this book home, get what you can out of it (and please don't pass over any other of my colleagues' worthy books), and the script that you write will be *read* and read by the people who matter: actors, talent agents, artists' managers, producers, and directors. If you're a student, your advisor will see a clear and sensible piece of work that has imagination and originality. If you're making your attempt with a real producer or buyer, you'll know if their notes are stupid or not. If you are an experienced professional and need to look at this whole thing from another perspective, you are as brave an artist as you need to be and I'm flattered at your attention.

I'll also help you write a likable script, which will get your next script to the right people even faster. Your script will be "industry ready."

I do guarantee that the script you learn to write from reading this book will not be stupid or embarrassing to you. It will be a script that works.

This book will ask you to work harder (not faster). It will help you find a way to write better, but not more. It will also ask that you come up with a personal way to actually anticipate the response to your work, both negative and positive. You will *know* what your script is, why you wrote it, and who the audience for it might be. You will know what's right about it, but more important, you will know what's wrong with it. And yes, there will be something wrong with it. After all, it's a work of art. But that's the whole deal with works of art. They perfectly express our human imperfection in a perfectly imperfect way.

There's no *one way* to write a story. If you took a survey of every great writer's methods and techniques, you'd get a list as different as each of their wardrobes. The person who tells you "This is *the* way to write a script" is like the person who tells you "My language is the only language to speak."

Certainly, any language must have nouns, verbs, and adjectives. Same with screenwriting. There are certain principles in storytelling that you simply can't do without, but somehow every script turns out differently.

When we write a story, whether it is prose, fact-based, or personal, we unconsciously observe many of the basic principles of storytelling. You do it every day.

A story is a carefully structured, sometimes spontaneously imagined piece of human craft. It's an amazing thing. We do it naturally and intuitively and we've been doing it for thousands of years. Yes, we understand in our hearts that the thoughtful and deliberate choices we make in the telling of a story are what make the story likable (or appealing or spellbinding or funny) — in short, entertaining.

These principles are simply natural to storytelling. We all know them, use them, and respect them. All of our favorite films, television series, and novels use these principles.

So you've been living with and using these principles all of your life. If you're interested in writing scripts, then you're probably even more conscious of these principles than you realize. You're already "breathing" them.

The principles we'll be working with in this book have all been extracted from the rich and long history of dramatic writing. Whenever we write a story we're paying tribute to Euripides, Shakespeare, Ibsen, and Shaw. The great novelists like Flaubert, Tolstoy, and Fitzgerald also observed these ages-old principles.

But rather than impose a set of rules on our work, we will use what naturally occurs in the process of storytelling that has worked through the millennia. We will codify it and make it like a list of "things to do"; "what to pack" before we can claim that our story is finished.

These fundamental principles of screenwriting upon which we build successful dramatic stories have been collected and distilled from a few other experts on screenwriting whom I admire: Robert McKee, Syd Field, William Goldman, Michael Tierno, and several of my colleagues at NYU, like Paul Thompson, or from UCLA, including Hal Ackerman. You should read all of their work as well.

I also urge you to examine as many different approaches as you can tolerate. I'm not a mind reader, but I can tell that this isn't your first and it won't be your last exploration of perfecting your craft as a screenwriter. It's not my last time either. No matter how long I've been doing this, I don't ever feel like I'm done learning about it. Every new script is a new experience — a new character, a new world, and a new story.

Even when you're working alone, screenwriting is collaboration. If it's not collaboration with all the dozens of craftspeople involved, it's collaboration with a part of your mind that thinks up the story. This is your silent partner who is in love with movies.

Using these fundamental principles, your story will finally achieve:

> **Unity** — The story is always being told.
> **Clarity** — The human value of your story is completely obvious.
> **Emotional impact** — It will be moving or funny or both. It will entertain.

These are the qualities that attract performers and other professionals to your script. If these people like it, it stands a much better chance of reaching the screen and/or earning you some money.

Most pleasant of all, you will actually enjoy re-reading your script, you will be in a position to fight for what's good in it, and you'll be more open to what needs changing. Because you will have structured it clearly, others will see the human value in it and will work along the same ideas that you have constructed, helping you to strengthen it.

Unfortunately, dramatic writing is not like cabinetry. However, as in cabinetry, there are fundamental principles of craft that we must follow in order to create a dramatic story; a story that does what it needs to do — *excite and engage the audience.*

Screenplays are not movies. They are carefully, thoughtfully, and deliberately written documents that *propose* the final movie, but must also evoke the great values and actions in the story.

These very talented people who make your movie are not simply interested in putting on a show and making a lot of money. I believe they are truly committed to using their artistic talents to illuminate a small part of the human condition.

BTW, if your script is not exciting to read, it will not be exciting as a movie — and I don't mean you're going to use exciting language. Producers, actors, everybody knows what an exciting script is and it has little to do with the language (while in a novel, language is almost everything).

The two major questions:

- Is the story always being told?
- Are we intensely interested in what the protagonist is going to do next?

In the 1930s, George Bernard Shaw, the leading dramatist of his generation, was lunching with Louis B. Mayer, founder of MGM Studios and, at that time, easily the most powerful man in movies (especially according to himself). Wanting to impress Shaw with his respect for aesthetics and high art Mayer expounded for some time on the subject of artistic values, showing off his knowledge while Shaw politely listened and chewed. When Mayer took a pause, Shaw was said to remark: "Mr. Mayer, that's all very admirable. But you're talking about art. I am here to talk about commerce."

More shocking news: the two are not necessarily mutually exclusive. Somehow, a myth has developed that the two are worlds apart. Certainly, there is a long history of films that were not very artistic but were nonetheless commercially successful. But, by and large, the most successful movies of the last one hundred years were both commercially and artistically successful.

Your script can be artistic AND commercial. This runs the full spectrum from *Dumb & Dumber* to *Chinatown* to *Breaking the Waves* to *The Sopranos* and long-running sitcoms like *Friends*. Good stories are simply *good* and appeal to a wide audience and continue to do so for very long periods of time. If you can still look at Da Vinci's "Mona Lisa" after 500 years, then let's admit it, that's some great work of art and, in its way, has been very commercially successful. The same thing applies to movies: if you can watch a film over and over again without getting sick of it (my minimum is ten times) then that movie is a damn good movie and goes on the permanent "art" shelf.

This Book . . .

The primary focus of this book is two-tiered.

My experience and my mentors have taught me a most important principle:

$$Story = Structure$$

That's because screenplays do not depend on "the writing" (language, style, voice, poetic ideas, grammatical mechanics) but on the structure (acts, scenes, lines of action — what's happening and what characters are *doing*).

Screenplays are like presenting your idea of a human being by only showing the skeleton except you're going to tell me, through the story, what this person will do when faced with certain choices.

That's action. That's the basic DNA of a story. The big question at every moment of your story, as your main character is faced with important choices:

"What's the hero going to do *now*?"

But where does this so-called "story" come from? Here's my answer:

Character = Story

That's what this book is about. After years of writing and teaching I have come upon an approach that I feel works for many writers, including me. It has also served me well as a teacher of hundreds of students including those at NYU's Undergraduate Film Program.

Create a central character who plays in great scenes and has a lot of problems to face — actively — *and you've got yourself a movie.*

These principles are the launching pad for your story. What your character does or doesn't do moves the story. Your story doesn't do anything without your main character being affected. But remember, you're not writing material to be read or enjoyed in people's minds while they're curled up on the sofa. You're writing material that is created to be performed.

If great scripts and stories were plentiful, then you wouldn't be reading this and there would be one hundred contenders for the Best Picture Oscar every year, not just nine. In fact, if things were different, we would almost never complain about seeing bad movies, sitting through boring plays, or reading lousy novels.

You wouldn't struggle for months or years writing a script, it would just tumble out of your brain like your grocery list. In fact, there would be no need for story departments, script development, and no one would need to read a script before it gets produced

— *there would be no rewrites!* What a world that would be! We could get out the crew and the equipment and just make a movie.

But that's not the way it is

The great Hungarian émigré producer Alexander Korda fled Nazi Germany penniless (with his Duesenberg limo, a chauffeur, and a valet), landed in England, and single-handedly created the British film industry. He had a famous sign hanging behind his desk that read: "It is not enough to be Hungarian — one must also have a good Second Act!"

Even Lars von Trier uses traditional structure in his films, as do David Lynch and Jim Jarmusch. They just do it in their own special ways.

Let's remember, a script is a naked, unadorned blueprint of a filmed screen story. It will be looked at, combed over, debated, hated, loved, and microscopically analyzed by about a hundred people before it gets produced and that's if you're on the fast track.

Unlike a novel or a ballet, it will enjoy the comments of these hundred people; their whims and opinions. And because they are paid to do it, they will make you change it. And if you can't (or won't) change it, they will hire somebody else who will. Let's not forget the generic name of your beloved script, the yield of years of labor, blood, sweat, and tears; your "baby." Industry big shots traditionally call it "The Property." And just like a piece of real estate, once it's got a new owner, that person can do anything they want from repainting the bedroom to gutting the kitchen. But I'm not saying you shouldn't be attached to it. Just know what's ahead of you.

You can't hide anything in a script like you can in a novel. Everything in your script is liable to cost some money. It's like the plans for a house, with each separate contractor asking, "What's this?" A movie script is scrutinized for quality, clarity, and cost as much as a fast-breaking news story is scanned for its accuracy. You can run, but you can't hide.

If there's something flimsy or questionable in your story, you will inevitably be exposed. If you're lucky, it happens before you start shooting. If you're not lucky, the audience will let you know in their own wonderfully ruthless way. If the owner — the studio, the network, or any producer — chooses to ignore a flaw in your story, don't think you've gotten away with something. They will pay in the end and they will blame the writer.

Ultimately, the audience will catch you and that'll be that. "I didn't believe he would go out with her, did you?" "How was he able to get that job so easily?" or "Can you actually obtain explosives by regular mail?" and hundreds of other comments that can doom a movie's credibility.

Movies, despite their belonging to what we call "popular culture," are thoughtful, deliberate, carefully arranged works of art. But they aren't like opera or classical music. They're more like good rock'n'roll; a folk art, but they are still important to our cultural and spiritual nourishment. Everybody loves the movies.

Your script will be read by an agent, sent to the story person at a film company, looked at by producers, directors, production designers, financiers, insurance actuaries, actors' managers, actors' personal story staff, the director's spouse — the list is very long. But the people I prefer to sell to, the people who I believe are *the* ones who decide if a picture gets made, are not the producer, the director, or the development person. I am writing my script for the person whose face gets blown up to the size of a billboard and is the last person to handle it as an artist. This person is the one whose face is up there and whose ass is on the playing field: the actor.

Along the way I will familiarize you with what we'll call the *moving parts* of your story. These parts are the things you cannot do without if you want to tell a good story.

If you were building a car, you'd need wheels, an engine, and a strong frame. If you were building a chair, it must be something people can sit in. However, isn't it amazing how many different kinds of chairs there are in this world? So you can be original. But these moving parts cannot be excluded. People need to be comfortable sitting in your chair.

I will make another promise:

> You get to *keep* everything in your story. Every crazy
> idea and wonderful quirky moment you want —

. . . but it has to work.

I call this *putting it in the box*. Don't get turned off. You will get to keep everything you've imagined in your script — but you have to "put it in the box." This script still has to turn out to be a recognizable story. It's a chair we can comfortably sit in or a car we can dependably and safely drive. I hope to give you an understanding of the true function of the characters, acts, scenes and scene structure, action, the beats (quanta of action), types of characters, the climax, what goes where — all that stuff.

Imagine your script as a wristwatch. It's a collection of all these unique moving parts, yet they are all working together to create a single experience — to tell the time. Your screenplay will be made up of different parts all unified in a single purpose — to tell the story.

My writing methods are pretty simple:

- Write everything . . .
- Write a lot . . .
- Make it into something . . .
- . . . and then rewrite it!

I want you to throw your clay onto the wheel and get going. I don't want you to justify yourself. That can get very depressing. It's the process of self-judging that's stopped many a story from being told.

You're going to stop sucking the wind out of your sails by pitching your idea at Starbuck's to your best friend who has no intention of supporting your effort. You're going to be discreet, professional, and, yes, thoughtful about your project. You're going to give yourself and your work the respect you both deserve.

You're most likely going to wind up stifling yourself if you sit down and ask yourself, "What's my story about?" That's a real buzz kill. Rather than interrogate yourself, I want you to *tell* yourself what you already know:

"There's this guy/gal and he/she is walking along one day and then — they are thrust into something that is really different and necessitates some kind of change." That's your idea; your pitch.

The rest is not so easy — but now, at least, you've opened the door. You with me? Let's get to it.

Chapter 1

FILM IS NOT A VISUAL MEDIUM

SO BACK TO THIS nearly blasphemous statement.

I'm not trying to eradicate over one hundred years of filmmaking or a tradition of the most visually stirring and beautiful films we've ever seen. I'm only trying to clear the brush, eliminate the mush, and call it like I see it.

But first you'll have to meet me halfway, abandon a few concepts you're stuck with about screenwriting (and movies altogether), and come along with me for the ride. Let's admit it: you're looking for help. Admitting you need help is the first step. Accepting help is your next step. With that, we'll be off on our journey just like in the movies.

Fundamentally, like a good story, it's all about change. Ironically, in order to change, you have to give up something to gain something.

I'm starting here because I want things to be clear right from the start. This is (hopefully) a way to view and understand movies and screenplays that will help you write them and write them better.

First, let's start by doing my favorite thing in writing: making sense.

If film really was a "visual" medium . . .

- Whenever we recommend or criticize a film, we would always talk about how "ugly" or "pretty" it is.

- Cinematographers, film editors, painters, sculptors, photographers, designers, and even choreographers would be the majority of successful filmmakers.
- Some of the greatest directors would not have risen from the ranks of writers and actors.
- Writers would not control every minute of the thousands of hours of television that we have watched and are watching now.
- We wouldn't sell written screenplays using language, based on a story, dialogue, character, and description. We would probably sell a movie as a graphic novel first.

But none of the above is the case.

And while some of our most gifted directors have in fact emerged from some of these professions such as cinematographers Ridley and Tony Scott, film editor Robert Wise, and even production designer Albert Lewin, the vast majority came from four very important branches of filmmaking:

Acting: Orson Welles, Robert Redford, Jon Favreau
Writing: Billy Wilder, Francis Ford Coppola, Charlie Kaufman
Directing: William Wyler, Martin Scorcese, D. W. Griffith
Producing: Cecil B. DeMille, Alan J. Pakula, Joseph
    Mankiewicz

Why?

I'm not trying to be crazy. I will say that film uses visual tools to tell its story. We would be nowhere without the whole cinematographic idea of films, its images, motion, and sound; the whole wonderful visceral experience of movies. And I will be the first one to say that *Gravity* would be nothing if it had never been a film.

But it's been a long time since audiences were simply held in thrall of the simplest kinographic qualities of film. After *The Sneeze* (1894) and *Train Enters a Station* (1895) everyone involved in filmmaking, including audiences, have been asking, "So what else have you got?"

Why?

Because we don't really go to movies simply because they look good, just as you wouldn't start a serious relationship with somebody simply based on their appearance (please, humor me!).

Let's agree that when we go to a movie, we want to feel something even if it's an avoidance of actual real-life emotional experience. We depend on movies to show us a story — hopefully one with some emotional content.

It wasn't long after these two early films that the visual tools of filmmaking were applied to drama; to the telling of a story about a character in order to excite the audience. In 1903 Edwin S. Porter released *A Day in the Life of an American Fireman* and suddenly everything changed. Using something called *film editing* (or in French, *montage*) Porter created the illusion of things really happening onscreen — physically, graphically, and emotionally. They were happening right now, in front of our eyes, with a level of excitement, both on screen and off, that had never been experienced before.

Audiences went nuts! (in a good way). Followed by *The Great Train Robbery*, anyone involved in movies immediately recognized that what had really been accomplished was a method of bringing stories, like plays on the stage, to the screen, but it was different.

While stage drama asks us to suspend our belief in an extreme way (after all, we're in the same room as Julius Caesar, yet surrender to the belief that he is actually murdered), movies suck us in. Movies conquer an audience like no other medium. For all intents and purposes, movies are real. And strangely, watching live human beings in theater, opera, dance, and the symphony is somehow artificial. Who can explain it?

So what kind of medium is film? We go to films primarily to see characters (played by good actors) get into and out of trouble (usually in that order).

So when taken as this hybrid package, I would say film is:

A STORY medium . . .
. . . where we experience PERFORMANCE of AN ORDEAL
(by actors) . . .
. . . moving through TIME.

Those are the three key elements of what makes film a very special hybrid medium. This is what I propose will keep you on track as you work on your script. It will, hopefully, keep you focused on the emotional, and not so much the visual — although, I promise, visuals will be there to use as you wish.

We go to the movies to observe a person in a narrative, which is an account of a human struggle that will excite us in some way. This includes comedies and documentaries. Every movie is developed and sold to the public as a terrific story with wonderful, well-known actors. They are *playing characters* — not simply striking poses or moving in shapes and rhythms. They are acting out a story that will make us laugh or cry or both.

And let's not forget the time thing. We mess around with time in movies more than any other medium. Certainly you can contain and manipulate time in novels and plays. But a movie has that special distinction of being able to entertain the audience with its treatment of time.

It's a wild kind of ride when you actually think about it. You sit there watching a story that takes place "now," yet it can, if it wants to, travel in any direction in time that's feasible and yet still have a beginning, middle, and end — and it isn't normally about time travel at all.

Memento proves this in spades. So does *Citizen Kane*. And in every way so does any other movie regardless of its treatment of time. As an audience we are utterly convinced that days, months, or years have passed, yet we're out of the theater in about two hours. Amazing. But that's not necessarily storytelling. That's just the miracle of drama.

These days the thing that drives me nuts, especially in teaching screenwriting in various higher institutions is that my students go to see perfectly lousy movies and they come into my class saying, "Hey — I can do *that*!"

But they're wrong. I assure you: those perfectly crappy screenplays were born wanting to be an Oscar winner. But a process occurred, almost like raising a sweet little baby who turns out to be a mass murderer, where all those involved took a silk purse and made it into a sow's ear. Nobody really intended to do it. It just happens. That's the sad part of our business and our craft. Good stuff gets ruined. Bad stuff gets made. It's just the way it is.

That's why when I teach I rarely if ever tell a student, "That's good" or "That's bad." My only criterion is "Does it work?" Like a chair, people have to be able to sit in it. Your screenplay must abide by certain recognizable qualities yet it can't go around copying every chair either. How do we do this?

It's funny how if you've never played a musical instrument or studied composition and music for years you never feel you could just sit down and write a symphony.

I'm not sure why, but people would never think of picking up a violin and expect to play Carnegie Hall. Or put on a tutu and start rehearsing *Swan Lake*. But for some strange reason, everyone who's seen a movie or watched TV thinks they can just sit down and write a script.

People suddenly wake up one morning, without any training in dramatic writing and say: "I'm gonna write and sell a screenplay! I've seen all these movies. If I just copy them, I'll be successful!"

Good luck.

Yes, screenwriting (and to a lesser extent playwriting) are "folk" arts. You don't need a PhD. Nobody who looks at your script asks, "Where'd you study?" You are not certified. There are no cumulative hours for a license (like an airlines pilot). You are free to do it in any way that gives you satisfaction.

But it helps to know what you're doing. Learning to write scripts is no different than any other craft. You learn the basics and start doing it. You compare your work to that of others around you and find out how good you might be. You might get produced. Or you might earn the support and recognition of other practitioners.

It takes time, training, diligence, and patience. You cannot just sit down and be good at it. I don't know a single TV or movie writer who just sat down and *did it* the first time out. I'm sure there are a few, but it's rare. And I don't teach rarity or genius. I do the nuts-and-bolts approach. I will guide you toward writing a script that's emotionally and intellectually satisfying; a script that makes sense and, above all, helps you see what it is that makes a script work.

So before you pick up that violin, let's take a few lessons first.

Why It's Taken You So Long to Write an Unfinished Script

This so-called script you've been working on for over *four years???* — that's a problem. I'm not talking about rewrites. I once spent over eight years on a script (not every day but stretched out over time). Working with a very smart director-producer friend, we kept over-hauling this thing to make it better. We also kept submitting it to studios and networks, getting feedback and using what we agreed on to improve the script. That's a terrific process in my opinion.

That's not what I'm talking about.

I'm talking about this project you keep going back to you that you're never satisfied with and that you probably haven't shown to anybody who knows what they're talking about.

Here's some idea of the actual timeline of a professional screenplay.

When a writer signs a Writers Guild of America (WGA) agreement to write a script, the first draft is usually due in about three months — "13 weeks." In other arrangements it might be six months. And in very rare situations, where there is a long-term development process, it will be delivered in one year. That's a first draft. Then it spends some time going through rewrites ("development"), sometimes with other writers, sometimes with the original writer(s); sometimes with a director or sometimes with a star and his/her development team.

There's a bit of a disclaimer here: the actual script can take 13 to 20 weeks. But if you are already doing what you're supposed to be doing you either know the whole story, from beginning to end, or you have actually created a *beat sheet* or a *treatment* that summarizes, scene-by-scene, the entire script *before you start writing that script.*

So it's not unreasonable for a buyer to think you can sit down and write it in a few months. And you can.

But first . . .

- You have to come up with the idea.
- Then make that idea "storyworthy" (keep reading . . .)
- Then, research and research and research your story (even if it's a comedy. Even if it's your own personal experience; even if it's all made up!).
- Then, create a beat sheet, step outline, or detailed treatment (all different versions of the same document)
- Then you sit down and write this nuisance of a document called a screenplay.

But if you haven't come up with a first draft in about a year, it's because you started out wrong and just went wrong-er. You put yourself on the wrong path and you just kept going and going and going. You lost your way and I assure you, you won't find your way back or out or any other "right" path because you weren't right to begin with. You didn't start off on the right foot and dozens of other euphemisms for "Go back to GO."

This is totally your fault!

But don't despair, you can totally fix it if you're willing to start at the beginning with your idea and then go through all the necessary steps to prove and exploit the most important property of your idea: Is it "storyworthy"? This is like "seaworthy" for a ship. Will it float? Does it work? Or will it sink the minute it's launched? Or will it just float around without going anywhere?

If You Feel Good Writing It, You're Doing It Wrong!

I believe that you're reading this book so I can save you a lot of heartache. And I apologize: I cannot advise you to simply sit down and write your script. If I did, you would write a pretty flimsy script, get it out there and wonder and worry why nobody is paying you an enormous sum of money for it.

Here's another strange thing to say: your idea doesn't need to feel good to you. That's right. Just because your idea doesn't get you excited doesn't mean it's bad. You shouldn't feel like it's going to be "fun" to write.

Sorry.

What your idea should feel is:

- Sound
- Solid
- Clear
- Compelling

That last word is the most important. It's a word that's thrown around a lot these days. You'll hear it from other writers, teachers, film people. "It's a compelling idea" or "That was a very compelling story." But that's a pretty fancy word for a medium as popular as movies.

What it means is this: it compels your audience to feel something or to know something that they came to your movie to feel and to know. This thing they get from your story isn't unfamiliar to them. In fact, it's pretty everyday. It's one of those values we listed earlier. It's something we all believe but for some weird reason, we never get tired of it. We like to see that belief reaffirmed over and over again. It is the feeling or the knowledge that your main character acquired in the process of going through your story.

That's right. It's not you (the writer) but you *talking through the main character* that got this story where it is.

It's not you saying, "I'm going to get this audience excited." It's you saying, "I'm going to show my main character going through something so compelling that my audience is going to thrill, laugh, gasp, or cry, or all of them." Through the experiences and responses of your main character, your audience is going to love (or hate) your movie. This is pure Aristotle.

Aristotle was a Greek philosopher, scientist, and thinker who lived from 384 BC to 322 BC, the golden age of ancient Greek culture. Aristotle was not an artist, he was someone who liked to study things and then come to profound conclusions. One thing he looked at very closely was drama (and comedy). Playwrights such as Euripides, Aeschylus, and Sophocles were still appreciated, decades since they passed away. They weren't the only playwrights. There were others. But these guys were the best. They were the Shaw, Ibsen, and Miller of their times. Their work had remained popular for almost one hundred years by the time Aristotle began studying why it was so damned good.

First thing he understood was that their work was compelling. Even though some of their stories were well known and many based on familiar ancient myths and folk history, audiences ate it up, over and over, generation after generation. Aristotle noticed how audiences flocked to see these plays while they stayed away from other playwrights and he asked himself "Why?" (He would have made a great studio executive! I think he would have loved HBO.)

He realized a few basic things:

- These stories were carefully put together so that they had an identifiable beginning, middle, and an end. An audience always knew what part of the story it was and Aristotle figured out this was just as important as what the audience was seeing performed.
- They all had vivid characters. In a few, there was always one main character, like Oedipus, who went through a remarkable ordeal, composed mostly of his own missteps, ending in a wrenching final moment of self-realization. The Greek word for this is *catharsis*. Its meaning is actually closer to "a purging" or a "release" of emotions.
- This he realized was the most important attribute of great drama: without the main character's ordeal, the audience would feel less, and that is what is called in show business "a flop."
- Finally, he stated very plainly what our job is as dramatists:

"Write what the story demands."

Think about that. It's not about you. It's not about "I'd love to see this on screen." It's not about, "wouldn't it be cool if . . . " He was telling us that it's about the protagonist. You, the writer, are telling this story because it must be told to the main character, not the audience.

So, what I strongly recommend is that you simply forget the audience. You actually don't know who this audience is. They number in the billions and for you to identify everything that amuses or moves or compels them as a group would not only be impossible, but incredibly time-consuming and ultimately stupid.

Forgive me. I just said you were stupid for considering the audience. I didn't mean that. I simply meant that for the time being, once you have come upon and created this marvelously storyworthy idea, then you must trust that you will now use the "moving parts" of your screen story to fulfill everything you hoped for in your audience's expectations.

I only ask that you don't keep them over your shoulder, laughing (or not) and applauding (or not). It's too damned noisy. You need to concentrate on your main character and his/her ordeal. You are permitted to understand why you as a writer have decided to do this to your character. That is vitally important. That is what makes you an artist. But don't get hung up on being "liked."

Aristotle also identified a great number of other attributes of great drama that we still use, whether we realize it or not:

- The **climax.** A Greek word, and yes, it's no coincidence that we use the word in relation to sex as well. It's just *the* most important, loudest, most exciting moment in a movie.
- **Protagonist** and **antagonist.** Two very important words in dramatic writing.
- **Prologue** and **epilogue**. One comes before your story begins, the other after it ends.
- **Praxis.** This was the word Aristotle used for action. Not a word we commonly use. It is all the stuff that happens and everything that the main character does.
- Aristotle also states something that I feel fully articulates the use of action:

"Drama is the psyche of the protagonist pushing outward."

Wow.

That to me is the essence of drama. The inner mind and soul of the main character made manifest through action. But what does that mean? Does that mean it's all the character's inner thoughts? No. Lots of dreams sequences? No.

Plain and simple, it's the actions that this character takes to get to the end of the ordeal. The things that are "pushing outward" are coming out as actions. Everything the main character does based on how he/she feels, which is in turn based on his/her response to the action preceding and the one after, etc.

Get it?

You Can't Learn to Write a Crappy Screenplay

If you haven't studied writing of any kind, this might be a difficult thing, this writing a screenplay.

Fundamentally we look at screenwriting the way we look at rock music. It appears that anyone really can sit down and write a hit song. They don't seem to need a college education. The Beatles barely made it out of high school. Carole King and all those Brill Building kids never got a degree in anything.

Since screenwriting can be classified as a "folk art," it springs from the people; from the folkways of down-to-earth philosophy and thinking that we are all a product of. But writing is a craft. Writing is a skill. Writing requires training. I would no more ask you to spit out a script than I would a mahogany shelf unit. You need to know some carpentry to do that. You need to know how to cut straight and how to use a hammer. Also, you need to lay out a good design plan if you're going to build a piece of furniture. Would you just pick up a hammer and saw and start building? No. You would measure the space. Make a drawing. Decide how much wood you'll need and then — *sticking to the plan* — set about to cut and nail and glue everything together. The more complex the project, the less confidence you'll have if you haven't had proper training and experience. Remember: you'll waste a lot of time, money, and wood if you don't know what you're doing.

Same with screenwriting. You have to know what you're making. You have to know the history of that thing you're making. You need to know the basis for two thousand years of dramatic writing and all that other stuff.

You Have to Know What You're Doing

Most screenwriters are pretty well-educated people. They know stuff like history and philosophy. I was raised in the theater; in show business. My parents were actors. My father appeared on Broadway and in films and on TV. He never studied anything! He dropped out of school in eighth grade. But, he was a standup comic for fifteen years before he started acting. He used his own senses to learn his craft.

Even though I was making films since the age of fourteen, I still went to NYU film school. I hated school, all of it. But sitting down and learning about literature was the most important thing I ever did. I thought I was going to be a director. I never thought of myself as a writer. But then, I started writing plays. They were easy to put on in New York. Two actors, a chair or two, some lights, a place for the actors to face an audience, and that is all that was needed.

But the thing is, I started studying how this is done. I read the great books. I read books on writing. I taught myself the craft. I used what I had learned in watching my father rehearse and perform. In short, I immersed myself in the world that I was hoping to succeed in.

You have to do the same. Writing a screenplay is no small task. I would say it's just about as hard as remodeling your kitchen or building a small house. It's no easier than writing a novel or composing a symphony. It's arduous work that requires knowledge and skill.

Notice I haven't even used the word *talent* yet. We will get to that.

Just as Brando dropped out of high school and came to New York to be an actor, he recognized immediately that he had to train and so (to also meet girls) he enrolled in training that would make him a skillful actor. He had talent. He had energy. He had a vision of himself as a successful performer. But he had to train.

I'll cut you a break: because you are reading this book you recognize your need to get more knowledge. To find out how other, more experienced writers do it. So you've taken an important step. You realize you need help. You understand that this thing may not be as easy as it looks.

As difficult as it is to write a script, it's not easy to sell one either. Notice I didn't say "good script." That's not only difficult, just as difficult as writing a bad script, but of the 287 people in the industry who are trusted to know such things, all of them are wrong at least 75% of the time. (PS: Okay, these numbers are arbitrary. But most of my colleagues would probably back me up.)

Imagine the movie trailer with Don LaFontaine saying in that deep rough voice: "In a world . . . where eighty-five percent of your output makes no profit . . . where those in charge of making the final decisions are wrong almost all of the time . . . a young writer decides to make his mark in a world where . . . NOBODY KNOWS ANYTHING! . . . coming this summer to a theater near you. 'NOBODY KNOWS ANYTHING!'"

That last phrase, coined by one of the greatest screenwriters of the past generation, William Goldman, sums it up completely. Expertise can only be measured by the most elusive methods. So it's almost impossible to "know" based solely on looking at a script if a movie is going to be any good or not. And if it's any good — will it make money?

Nobody actually "knows-knows." It's full of unknown-unknowns (sounds like Donald Rumsfeld!). That's because it is just as surreal. Most moviemakers simply look at a script and decide: "This is worth doing. I believe there's a decent-sized audience out there for this. And I believe a few good actors will be interested in doing it." That is the most substantial moment in the inception of a film. That's when it begins. The years-long trek toward the completion of a feature-length motion picture begins because somebody really wants to make it.

You have probably seen a bunch of unimpressive movies. They may not have been horrible, but they weren't great. You also saw a few great movies, movies you really loved. You're probably thinking, "Well, I don't think I could write that really great movie. But I'm pretty sure I can write that slightly crappy movie I saw and get some money for it. Maybe that would start my career as a screenwriter."

'Scuse me?

First of all, if your first movie is crappy, it will most likely end your career, not start it. The stories behind what happens to perfectly good scripts on their way to becoming a movie would fill another few books. Some of those stories are contained in the remarkable memoirs written by William Goldman. He's a great screenwriter. He has written award-winning scripts and also scripts we'll never see and at least one that really flopped. But he was convinced, in his amazing Oscar-winning mind, that these would be great scripts. That's just the way *you* have to feel. He'll be the first and not the last person to tell you: "We work just as hard on the bad ones as we do on the good ones."

So first, before you start writing crap, you have to know what you're doing. Only the best singers can actually deliberately sing off-key (and often for comic effect).

This means humbling yourself to the task, understanding what "mastery" of this craft actually means, and applying your knowledge to a professional working life — even if you're not earning any money at it. So relax. Open your eyes, your ears, and your soul. You'll get there if you take the necessary steps.

There's No Such Thing as a "Bad Idea," Only a Story Poorly Told

Story ideas can be tricky things. Sometimes an idea seems great because you have the potential to surprise the audience at the end (*The Sixth Sense*). Sometimes an idea can be a way of telling an utterly familiar story, yet it can contain nagging anticipation (*Titanic*). Or sometimes an idea can be just a value; simply a human emotion, like "madness" (*Repulsion*) or "lost in space" (*Gravity*) or "you can't win against real power" (*Chinatown*).

Tips
- "Don't try to be clever."
- "Don't struggle to be original."

Clever is simply a way of tricking the audience. That's fine, but you can only do that trick once. That's what "spoiler alerts" are about. A "one-trick" movie is simply that. And believe me, you're welcome to try. There are many satisfying experiences from these one-trick movies. Yes, *The Sixth Sense*, because both Bruce Willis and the audience reach their understanding at the same moment. But it's an amazing value in the end. The main character learns to live with the truth about himself.

But who wants to write a movie that can only be seen once?

Then there's *Psycho*. Forgive me for defying the cult of adoration around this movie. Hitchcock is a genius. An absolute master of filmmaking. But where the heck did that come from? And who is the main character in that movie anyway? In my opinion Hitchcock doesn't so much resolve that story as simply put an arbitrary surprise on the end and then wrap it up with a pipe-smoking psychiatrist. I believe that Aristotle would have called this *deus ex machina*. This was an actor who was lowered on a mechanical platform, imitating a god (for authority) and explaining the story to the audience because the story couldn't explain itself.

Fundamentally, if you can't explain the story to yourself, who else will understand it?

So many of my students say, "I've got it all in my head, but I can't explain it. Just let me write a script and it'll all be clear."

Don't kid yourself. Nothing's clear until it hits the page.

Creating your story is the process of creating *clarity*. Every movie you've ever loved is clear. Its story, its main character, and its value are always crystal clear. And yet, they appear to be "original" (they're not) and they appear to be "clever and surprising" (not really) and they are said to be "subtle" (well, sort of). But when you go out afterward with your date or your friends and discuss it you will always agree on major points of that movie. You will agree on what happened (that's the plot) and you'll agree on what it's about (that's the story). That's because everything about it is clear.

Good movies are thoughtful works of art. They have to be well thought-out because if they weren't, then there would be a lot of money wasted. Wouldn't it be great if you could just get out there with a camera and a cast and a crew and just mess around until you came up with something? I did that when I was in high school using an 8mm home movie camera. It was great. And then I'd get the film back from the lab and I would scratch my head, not being able to figure out what went wrong.

I didn't have a script. I didn't have a main character. I didn't have a story. Fundamentally I had a lot of exposed film, but I didn't have anything resembling a movie. That's how I learned. Although I went on to make some fairly abstract adolescent movies in high school (hey — it was the '60s!) I still had a script whenever I went to make my little movies. That helped me plan my movie so I could call a friend and say, "Hey, it'll only take a couple of hours because I only need you do this part of my script." Rather than, "Hey, we're going to go out with my camera today and mess around and I have no idea what we'll be doing."

Which makes more sense?

This struggle is shared by everyone who makes a movie or tells a story. Jim Jarmusch shares it with Sidney Lumet. David Lynch shares it with Martin Scorcese.

So, even though you're a gifted artist, you must set out to create something that is clear and must in some way do something very important. This thing that we're all struggling to do:

It's gotta make sense.

Your story must be coherent, cohesive, and in its own way, make its own sense. *The Sixth Sense* makes its own special sense according to the rules of the living afterlife. *Star Wars* makes sense in its own interplanetary Federation v. Empire thing. And certainly we accept everything in *Gravity* even though I'm not sure you can hop from space station to space station as if they were rest stops on the interstate. But the movie made sense.

Most of all, what you're focused on as an audience (and you will be as a screenwriter) is the struggle of your character through whatever ordeal you're putting him/her through. That's your initial concern. That's the first thing that will determine if your story is working:

Before this thing is over, what will this cost the character?

In *The Sixth Sense*, it costs him his marriage, his relationships, his life. In *Star Wars* Luke Skywalker must sacrifice everything, be humiliated by Yoda, lose his hand — and still do the right thing, kill his father (I really like that one!). Yet, it all makes sense.

So, one of the first things that should occur to you is what kind of ordeal you're going to put your character through. But how do you think that up?

One thing you have in common with your audience; the quality that you are certain to share with all of them; the only predictive factor you can rely on; that one thing that you can dependably say you share with any moviegoing audience:

You're *human.*

Your story will be about a human being. Even if it's about a fish (*Finding Nemo*) or a baby deer (*Bambi*) or a group of toys (*Toy Story*) or a hobbit (*Lord of the Rings*) or a hero with superpowers (*Superman, Spiderman*), your story will be about *a person* struggling with something important.

This important struggle will be generated from what appears to be the normal, everyday things in life: Work? Love? Adventure? Or how about Fear? Greed? Loss? These are all human conditions and circumstances that allow us to identify with some common human value. Something that we all think about. Something that we may have actually struggled with ourselves. Some of us may have been successful in this struggle. Others failed. But whatever it is, it's what the story is about. It's why we came to see this movie (besides the thrills, the laughs, and the emotions).

In the end, there are only a few possible outcomes for your story:

- "Wow! The hero really did it!" (happy ending, *Gravity*)
- "Oh no, the hero really messed up. That's too bad." (sad ending, *Chinatown*)
- "Oh well, even though the hero didn't succeed, I bet they learned something from this experience."(ironic ending, *The Sixth Sense*)

Believe it or not, any of these three might be the "motor" of the movie you just liked or what's inside the idea you're trying to develop right now. Whatever the case, you will need to know this at some point in your process before you go ahead with that script.

What I mean is, you can write a script right now if it makes you happy. But you'll still have to go through it and make it something of value. Something that tells us about your character's problem, his/ her struggle and why you are putting your character through this ordeal.

This is what gets you and any other movie audience excited.

So, first big question:

Does your idea generate value?

A human value is simply something that we believe and we want to reaffirm by means of telling our story. That's pretty simple. All decent movies, even the *The Fast and the Furious* series, generate a human value. How about the movies we're watching today? Here, in one short statement each, is the dramatic and emotional value of these Oscar nominees:

Gravity: Under the worst kind of pressure, you can find within you the will to survive. She's under time pressure, a threat to her life, and she has a problem in her head about her dead daughter. All are important in the story.

12 Years a Slave: A man's freedom shouldn't be taken for granted. Sometimes you have to fight for it! He's trapped, can't get out, and doesn't want to die trying.

American Hustle: Friendship, trust, and love are much more important than money.

Blue Jasmine: Not facing the truth of your life is a disaster. People may lie in order to get the big score, but in fact they only need to empathize with and love each other to have what really matters.

Captain Phillips: We need to be prepared that on certain days, things can go horribly wrong. The routine of life is sometimes a dangerous experience.

Dallas Buyers Club: The path from selfishness to compassion is a worthwhile struggle. But first, you will have to face your mortality in order to see the truth of yourself.

EXERCISES

Fill in the value statements for the following other Oscar nominees:

Her
Nebraska
Philomena
The Wolf of Wall Street

Now make your own list of six movies (hopefully, movies you like!) and fill in the value statements.

_____

_____

_____

_____

_____

_____

Make the value statement about your current project. If you're stumped, make it a longer list and see which statement is the strongest.

_____

_____

_____

_____

_____

_____

....

Chapter 2

SCREENPLAYS ARE NOT WRITTEN — THEY'RE BUILT

Stories Are Energy Machines

Stories — especially screenplays — are energy machines. All of the energy, time, effort, and passion you have written into your script is just sitting there on the page waiting to be unleashed on the world. All those hours and days and months and years you've spent working and worrying, all the frustration and thought that came out of your psyche has now been condensed into this code known as writing. With any luck, it will be interpreted by a whole group of other artists and craftspeople.

Hopefully, a studio, network, or company in the form of an executive producer will take up the project. They will plan to make money with your script. They will hire others — a vast creative team — who will translate your script into a photographed product.

Now even more energy is being expended on your story.

So it all gets reduced into this little frame   and *wham*   it all comes out for the audience, who then translate all of that invisible energy of thought and craft into some kind of experience.

That's a movie!

Your story is like one of those rubber-band-powered toy airplanes.

Over the time of your story, you're going to wind that rubber band so tight that when you let it go — the climax of your story — it's going to go zoom! (More on this later!)

But how do you do that on paper using a format so ugly and without the freedom of a novelist?

How do we create this energy?

We already understand that we are creating a system of "values." The beliefs and truths that we find to be universal for all sentient beings. Anyone who can experience a complex story can experience and share these fundamental human values.

But how do we take these towering values and translate them into drama? How do we get this stuff on the page?

There Are No Rules in Screenwriting — But You Have to Obey Every Single One!

You'll probably read other books on screenwriting. I actually know some of those writers and teachers. I can call them at home!

So, going under the premise that "Nobody knows anything" we can further extrapolate, "Everybody knows something." You can credit that to me. Probably one of the stupidest things I've ever said. But I feel it opens the door to the very thing that scares or thwarts people when they sit down to write a script: "What am I supposed to do now?"

It's funny, Robert McKee hates to call them "rules." He prefers the term *principles*. It is satirized so wonderfully in Charlie Kaufman's script *Adaptation*. Fundamentally, rather than follow a bunch of rules — like laws — let's obey certain concepts because they've been shown to work. I like that.

But I would much rather be able to stop somebody on the street for spitting because it's a rule rather than expect them to obey the "spirit" of the law and the principles of decency. Who's kidding whom? *You must have a minimum set of elements in a story or it's not a story.* That may have been based on the spirit of principles at one time, but I really accept it as a rule now. So here are some really fundamental rules that you must follow or you go to screenwriting jail:

1. "I will begin a story only with a single main character."

That's a rule. I obey that rule. I think you should too.

2. This character will take a journey or experience an ordeal that will deliver him/her to a new idea of him/herself and his/her life.

I obey that rule too.

3. I believe you should not place anything in the story that isn't put there without careful thought and consideration and is a chosen part of the design of that story.

These are my primary rules. I believe if you simply obey — and never break — these rules, you will be well on your way to telling a good solid story that works. So shoot me — there actually is some minimum of rules you have to obey. If you treat them as "principles" I believe you'll cut yourself too much slack. These are the deal-breakers.

Screenplays Are Like Good Watches: The "Moving Parts" of a Screenplay

When we look at a watch, we only see the time. But, no matter what kind of watch you use, digital or analog, old or new, accurate or not, you depend on that watch to tell you the time. You don't actually care how. You only care that it's giving you what you want when you want it. But behind that face or LED is a complex, interdependent system that makes that thing work. But it's hidden by the actual product that we get from this machine. It looks like one thing — but it's really a bunch of moving parts.

Most importantly, I believe that no watchmaker worth his weight puts anything inside a watch that isn't there for a damn good reason. No part goes unused; no unnecessary part is ever included — there simply isn't room!

It's the same with a story or a screenplay — all of it. If you follow the rules that govern the making of a watch, I don't think you can go wrong.

The beauty of a screenplay is that all that structural material, all those tricks, all that stuff is actually invisible. The thing that you get from a movie is the *experience*. The thrills. The laughter. The tears. If you're a typical moviegoer (i.e., not working in show business), you don't see any of that stuff that we're talking about here.

But any audience will react to something that doesn't work. Just as they would recognize that a clock was broken. Or they couldn't read the dial. Audiences intuitively and subliminally know what's going on in a movie because they are involved in the experience.

If it gets too slow, they stop getting excited. If the story is not being delivered in a certain way, they get mad! If things go radically counter to expectations, or worse, if they go exactly as expected, they will hate the movie! Audiences may excuse a corrupt politician or drug-addicted movie star, but any movie that doesn't deliver — fugeddaboudit! An audience will dismiss it like yesterday's cheesecloth. They will even tell their friends, "Whatever you do — don't see this movie! It stinks!"

Merciless!

But when they're right, they're right.

This is because just as we can tell when a watch is broken, most people can see that a movie doesn't work. They couldn't tell you exactly why. But that doesn't matter. If your watch doesn't work, they're gonna find one that does.

Same with producers, directors, actors, and other industry professionals.

What I propose is that you see your script like a watch. Precise. Designed. Composed of interlocking moving parts that all contribute to the illusion of one thing — *unity,* as Aristotle would call it.

Unity means everything's working like a team toward a common goal. It means that each part is used for its specialty. No part is unused. No part is unnecessary or gratuitous. Pay really special attention to that last statement. Keep these words ringing in your head (like the dream sequence in *Vertigo;* words echoing deep in the dark limbo of your brain):

"Unnecessary . . . Gratuitous . . . Unnecessary . . . Gratuitous . . ."

We will look at a screenplay and its underlying story as we would a well-tooled machine. It must fulfill a certain output. It is built well. It functions beyond expectations. Those who put it to use, enjoy the way it feels — balanced, well-shaped, familiar . . . yet different.

But here's why screenplays are the weirdest document ever created.

A writer must take an enormous philosophical impact and a profound emotional experience and reduce it to:

"INT. LIVING ROOM - NIGHT".

Isn't that weird? Why is that?

Money.

That's right. The only reason we use this highly specialized format that looks more like an engineering document than writing, is so that time, location, and labor can be systematically distilled for about two hundred people who will be involved in the actual manufacture of the final product.

From the story department to the studio exec, to the director, to the actors, to the crew, to the postproduction crew, to the mixer, to the distributor — they all have to look at something that tells *what, where, when, who,* and *how.* Then they can determine "how long" and "how much." Then the movie goes into production.

"Art," right?

Yes. It is art. It's a hybrid art that involves writing, acting, photography, audio, design, painting, clothing, military logistics, transportation, financing, and marketing. But have no doubt it is art. And without the artists, it's nothing.

Because it uses visual tools to tell its story, those visual elements in screenplays have actually decreased over the years. You don't even see "CUT TO:" in most screenplays anymore. So your story is told with language. But being a "great" writer may not matter. However, you really do need to know how to write. More importantly, what you really need to know is how to put things together. You need to know how to build a good story. Like a good watch, your script is useful, meaningful, beautiful, and it works.

So your great idea ends up like a good watch. That's the first elementary step in putting your thoughts down on paper and "gettin' this thing on the hump!" (Major King Kong, *Dr. Strangelove . . .*).

CHECKLIST The Moving Parts of Screen Story

☐ **A SINGLE MAIN CHARACTER** who is the primary point of view of the story. We start with this person. We end with this person. It is the experience of this character that gives the story action and meaning.

☐ **A BEGINNING, MIDDLE, AND END** (or Act I, II, and III). These three sections, unequal in length, represent three escalating stages of the story.

- In Act I: A main character, with certain problematic traits (a *character deficit*), has a difficult task ahead of him/her that must be resolved. This sends the character on an ordeal or a journey.
- Act II is the journey and the ordeal leading to a moment when "all is lost" (sound familiar?), where it appears that the character cannot (or will not) resolve the problem.
- Act III is the time when the character must make a choice to a) resolve the problem and change, or b) to arrive at a point of recognition about life and his/her problems or c) be defeated by the problem.

☐ **INCITING INCIDENT:** (in Act I) A seemingly ordinary, everyday act that brings the character into the stream of the story: a job interview; a phone call; meeting someone at a bus stop. In Chinatown it's when the phony Mrs. Mulwray comes to Gittes' office. This is an ordinary, everyday thing for Gittes. In *Being John Malkovich* it's when Craig Schwartz (John Cusack) goes for the job interview at LesterCorp, which is on the 7 1/2 floor of an office building. This happens on the top of page 8—the 7 1/2 page, which is 7 1/2 minutes into the movie — which is Charlie Kaufman's way of messing with our heads! It's an in-joke about the fact that we screenwriters are pestered by mythical rules that say: "You have to have this on page 8!" Thanks, Charlie Kaufman.

☐ **CALL TO ACTION:** This is the action that the character must take in order to start the journey. In most movies the character is forced into this action by the circumstances built up in those previous beats, but directly attributable to the inciting incident. In *Chinatown* it's when Gittes gets his nose slashed by "the midget" (director Roman Polanski). Now Gittes must take action! And it's because he's been led to go there at the behest of the phony Mrs. Mulwray. Now the real ordeal begins. In *Malkovich* it's when

Craig meets Maxine (Catherine Keener). No — it's not when he gets sucked into Malkovich's head! That's also Kaufman's way of messing with us. Craig's story goal is to get Maxine in bed. The Malkovich thing is just a cool way of luring her.

☐ **OBSTACLES, PROBLEMS, AND NEW RELATIONSHIPS:** This is Act II. These will be consistent with your character's journey. In mythology, Jason has to go get the Golden Fleece. He's beset by all sorts of disasters and tests to his character and his skills. Same with your movie. In *Chinatown* Gittes gets involved with the real Mrs. Mulwray, first as an adversary, then as a lover. He meets and goes up against her father, Noah Cross, the most powerful man in Los Angeles. Additionally, there are a variety of characters and situations that bring Gittes into a crisis, make him face his past, and, in the end, bring him face-to-face with his worst human problem.

☐ **CLIMAX:** The biggest, most important moment in the story that releases the character from the journey and the struggle. However, this character must still move on to one more step . . .

☐ **THE RESOLUTION:** The character either resolves to change or recognizes the need to do so. In a tragedy the protagonist is left with either the folly or horror of his/her deeds. Oedipus plucks out his eyes he's so pissed off at himself!

These elements will cause an engagement in your audience and will result in an emotional reaction to your story. This is known as the *catharsis*, a meaningful emotional response. I believe it's not so much a purging as it is a movement within a person's psyche.

Finally, you need to set up two key questions for your story:

1. What is your character's "path to satisfaction"? In *Chinatown* it is Jake Gittes' drive to bring down Noah Cross and expose

the land-grab scheme that will steal the city's water supply. This "Path to Satisfaction" is a lousy idea for the protagonist, but he/she doesn't know that. It's the thing they must do to get satisfaction. It's not until the end of the story that they understand what they should have done in the first place!

2. What is the real change your character experiences? Jake Gittes learns that he's cursed with a good heart and a lousy head. He's done this before; he's tried to do good, but it ends up hurting someone close to him. And now, once again, tragedy. "Forget it, Jake. It's Chinatown," as one of his associates tells him. It's *you* (the main character) . . . and you can't do a damn thing about it.

And here is what I call the screenwriter's mission. This will make the conflict in your story continuous and create the tension you need to keep the energy level going. Put this somewhere visible or get a brass plaque made and hang it near your workspace (I would recommend tattooing it to the backs of each hand, a la *Night of the Hunter*):

Your protagonist struggles for satisfaction (the "plot")
but . . .
the writer is going to
teach this character a lesson that will last (the "story").

"Putting It in the Box": A Screenplay Is Like a Chair — You Gotta Be Able to Sit in It!

Everybody knows how a movie works. There's a beginning, a middle, and an end. A good story. Humor me and forget about watches. Let's talk about furniture. A good story is like a good chair. It has legs. It has a seat and a back; sometimes it has arms. But fundamentally, anybody who uses it needs to sit in it. Some are more comfortable in your chair than in others. That's the way it goes sometimes. But when you're looking for a good chair, you really know what you're looking for. You're not looking for something you cannot sit in! You will choose the one that's as comfortable as you can find and/or fits in with your home or office.

Same with your story. It needs to be identifiable as a story. It must adhere to the ages-old requirements that have worked for over two thousand years.

It also has to be different enough for people to say, for example: "I'm excited at this new approach to *Romeo and Juliet*. How's this sound: New York's Hell's Kitchen, the 1950s, Puerto Rican and white teenage gangs killing each other for supremacy in a run-down urban neighborhood. But the love affair between two of them causes tragedy." Or, "I like this bank robbery movie about a guy who just needs one last score and then he'll marry the neighborhood girl he's been in love with since grade school."

Sure, we've seen them before. Yet, we can create variations on these stories ad infinitum. A chair is a chair, yet there are so many different kinds of chairs!

So, don't *not* make any old chair. But make *your* chair and make a chair that works.

This is something I call "Putting It in the Box." It means you must create a recognizable story. The script must have the traditional elements that all stories are made up of. Like a chair: legs, a seat, and a back. When someone reads your script he/she will say, "It's a script. There are problems we need to fix, but on the whole, this is a sound story with recognizable elements."

Sorry. Am I strangling your creativity? Let's get something straight. Painters need to put their pictures in a frame. It can be a still life of fruit or the most abstract collection of splatters and lines, but they need to put it in "the box." You cannot paint everything. You cannot write everything.

Without these structural restrictions all art would be a never-ending torrent of emotion and ideas with nothing to bring it meaning.

That is what artists do: they bring meaning to particular elements of the world that get their attention. They think about it profoundly, then they express something that will bring the viewer's attention to it. But they have to put it "in a box." Into a frame, up on a pedestal, onto a stage, or onto the screen — that's a pretty limited box. Yet you can almost fit the whole Arabian Desert on it. Or the wing of a fly. But it's still *in the box.*

These restrictions are actually blessings in disguise. Rather than all of your ideas coming out into a waterfall of chaos, it's like a water hose. That hose, that nozzle, creates the pressure you need to use the water properly — whether it's to put out a fire or water your flowers. Without these restrictions you simply couldn't do it.

This is what I have created as the "Three Actions of Art." I believe that all arts share these common goals in expression. In order to create your work of art — your screenplay — you should be aware of them.

Your goals as an artist are:

1. **To get attention.** The primary goal is get your viewer's or audience's attention. This is how all advertising is designed. In fact, which industry employs more "artists" by title than any other? Advertising. They're smart. They hire artists, designers, and writers to get consumers' attention. But that's all they do. Advertising does not have the next two elements, which will create a real work of art.

2. **To give meaning to the ordinary.** This is easy. Who took Campbell's soup cans and made them into the most historically important work of art since the "Mona Lisa"? Andy Warhol. He proved that all an artist needs to do is find the ordinary and get our attention. His cans made him millions of dollars. He started a movement called Pop Art. He fathered the modern art movement that dominated the

second half of the twentieth century. And in movies, TV, and drama, we are engaged by stories that are, for the most part, fairly ordinary. Boy meets-girl, family problems, bank robberies, earthquakes, tsunamis, and the struggles of humanity. None of them have any meaning and they happen all the time. But *you* are going to select something that holds your own interest and tell us a story about it and in doing so you are on your way to creating a work of art. But you need one more action before you're done.

3. **To provide imaginative access to another consciousness.** Huh? Sorry, this sounds heavy and intellectual, but it too is very familiar. Whenever an artist sets out to create something, he/she is automatically exercising his/her imagination. That's a given. You have an idea about a bank robbery story, so you are going to use your imagination, plus your intellect, to tell this story. Same with a painting, sculpture, play, or ballet. But you are providing a unique point of view simply by virtue of the fact that *you* are creating this work of art. This is "another consciousness." Sure, it may appear to be from the main character's point-of-view. Or it may look like the portrait of a lady almost smiling. Or it may be a rousing symphony. But it's all from one person's head — yours. And that makes it unique. That lets your audience see something they've never seen before and to experience a story they've never experienced before that makes a point that will enhance their view of the world.

I have a deep and abiding belief that all arts share the same mission and this is how I choose to describe it.

You are going to try to adhere to the proven structural and artistic principles that have governed all art since the beginning of human creativity. This holds true for *The Hangover* as well as *Melancholia*.

Whatever it is, it's always doing what art does: reaffirming our view of humans in this world.

You're pretty impressive, being an artist. I hope you can think of yourself as part of a vast, global community, holding up a mirror to show us how we are often noble, always foolish, and sometimes evil. You've got a terrific resource to tell great stories: people — even if they're fish, baby does, or dinosaurs.

So how are you going to fit this thing into "the box?"

The World of the Journey Is the Plot!

I'm as lazy as most people, so I like to keep things easy when I first start a new project. I like to know what I'm in for before I really get going with the creative (and arduous) task of a new script. I don't remember completing any full-length project in less than two years. So I like to have my story ducks in a row as I enter this unknown territory of my new project.

Of course, the first thing you need — the must-have — is a main character (more on this in the next chapter). Know this character, even if he or she is completely made up. If you're working in the best way, you will be drawing this character's traits from real-life characters in your life. It could be your best friend in high school, one of your relatives, or someone you worked with who was memorable to you.

With this character comes the problem: this person is habitually unsuccessful at something in life, yet he/she appears to be successful at something else. In *The Godfather* Michael is a successful American citizen, but he's not a successful son. In *Chinatown* Jake Gittes is a successful sleazy private eye, mostly doing divorces. But he's hugely unsuccessful at relationships, which we learn as the movie progresses.

Whatever it is, I call it the *character deficit*, a problem that keeps his/her life from being whole.

Once you decide on this, you can skip to the next shortcut (and the last, I'm sad to say). It's a two-part shortcut:

1. What unfamiliar world are you going to take your character through?
2. What human value lies at the end of your story? What lesson, connected to this character's deficit, will be revealed to the character at the end of your story?

In *Midnight Cowboy* our hero decides that he's going to leave his middle-of-nowhere Texas town to go to New York City where he will become the most successful male stud prostitute. Wow — what a terrific idea — not for him, but it's a great idea for a story about him.

Jake Gittes in *Chinatown* decides to a) take the bait from the Mrs. Mulwray imposter and b) sue whoever attacked him and in doing so bring down the land-grab scheme of Noah Cross. Again, another really bright idea from our so-called hero. It will only end in tears, pal.

In both cases these characters are pushed onto a journey that produces the ordeal that makes up the largest part of your story: Act II, or as it is referred to by many screenwriters, "The Beast."

So here's my trick (and you'll probably say, very sarcastically — "Some trick! Where'd you learn that — from a dead person?") But the trick is to choose the world that will a) present this character with the most obstacles and b) teach the character his/her lesson.

In *Maria Full of Grace* a seventeen-year-old Colombian girl who works at a factory realizes she's pregnant by the boy that she does not love. But her problem is that she's stubborn, willful, and impetuous. She really doesn't do well with authority. She's defiant. So what lesson will she learn? Her choices in life are meaningful. Why? Because she's about to be a single mom!

This is not an unusual story. *Juno* tells almost the same story with almost the same circumstances.

But in *Maria*, writer-director Josh Marston takes his character and his audience on an amazing journey: the world of female Latin American drug mules. These are young women, who by their appearance do not arouse suspicion as international drug couriers. They are paid good money to swallow drugs wrapped in condoms and travel to faraway cities to deliver the stuff.

Cool journey, huh? And what does it have to do with pregnancy or marriage or getting along with people? Well, actually, not much. But in the process our hotheaded Maria must learn to survive completely on her own and soon realizes that her general attitude needs to be knocked down a notch or a) she can get killed or die accidentally from the swallowed stuff and b) she has to make real choices now, not for herself, but for her baby.

In the story, Maria quits her very valuable but slave-like job, alienates her family, and breaks up with her boyfriend. She is then recruited by a guy who combs the countryside luring vulnerable young people into the trade. The combination of his charm, Maria's inflated sense of self-determination, and her momentary economic vulnerability allows this story to take hold with a remarkably logical cause-and-effect.

And so the journey begins.

This journey takes us step-by-step through the world of international drug mules. From Maria's recruitment to her meeting a more experienced "mentor" woman who teaches her some of the tricks of the trade; to the swallowing of the drugs, through her travel to the US, through seeing another mule busted and almost getting busted herself; through death (of her mentor); then stupidly running from her keepers, then trying to survive in New York; learning what it really means to be a woman, and ultimately making the final decision in one of the most subtly moving endings in movie history (in my opinion).

Good story, well told. And the movie is good too!

In the case of *Maria* she not only journeys through a completely unfamiliar world of people and events, but to another country and its most complex and intimidating city, New York (a journey unto itself, I assure you).

However, in *The Godfather, Chinatown,* and *Three Days of the Condor* each protagonist is actually taken on a journey through a world they should be completely familiar and comfortable with, but in these stories, their choices have caused a new circumstance that transforms these comfortable and familiar worlds into challenging and dangerous places.

Whatever the case, it's a place that is no longer *easy* for the character.

That's the key: difficulty. The tricky part: forcing your character to actually decide to put him-/herself through it!

In *Midnight Cowboy* it's the world of New York's Times Square — lowlifes, pimps, drug addicts, and street people.

In *The Godfather,* intrigue and death in the world of the top level of the Corleones and the other Mafia crime "families."

In *Chinatown,* 1937 Los Angeles, but as seen as plunder for the rich and powerful.

In *Condor* it's New York City, but not the one that Joe Turner knows. It's a New York where he is now the hunted and by the very people who are his employers!

In *The Hangover* it's Las Vegas and the Nevada desert wilderness.

In *The Visitor* it's the world of US immigration and illegal immigrants.

In *Get Him to the Greek* it's the world of Aldous Snow, a degenerate egomaniacal rock star and a global journey that goes from LA to London to Las Vegas to LA.

So what's the trick?

Fundamentally, this "world" and the journey through it will serve as your plot.

But wait a second — isn't "plot" the same as "story"?

I don't think so. And keeping them as separate terms (but not separate entities) helps me define my story.

- Your plot is what happens.
- Your story is the human value.

Once you decide on what story you're going tell, fill in these statements:

"It's about this guy/gal who ultimately understands

_____."
        [human value]

"The plot takes him/her through the world of _____

_____."
        [world of story]

Always remember that the world you take them through, even if it's their own home (*Poltergeist*), their own family (*My Big Fat Greek Wedding*) or their workplace (*9 to 5*), is a world that is as unfamiliar to this character as it is to your audience.

EXERCISE

- What's your protagonist's life problem (*character deficit*)?
- How do the succeeding events (*moving parts*) force your protagonist to take the journey (*inciting incident* and *call to action*)?
- What world are you taking him/her through? How will it test his/her psychic and spiritual strength?

Why Now?

This is one of a group of questions we need to ask before we get going.

If you're going to put your character through this arduous ordeal, testing all of the resources of his/her spirit and his/her resolve in order to teach him/her some profound human lesson, WHY TODAY?

Many of my stories, those of my students, and those of the movies that I've seen, fail or succeed on this all-important question.

Let's look at some of our standard examples.

Three Days of the Condor: because Joe Turner's casual investigation of the possibility of an "inner" CIA network has been discovered and he and his colleagues have been targeted for assassination. But he's going to learn that you don't fool around with the CIA. He tells his boss, "I actually trust some people." That's a problem when you work for the CIA!

Maria Full of Grace: because she's pregnant and lost her job and is offered what appears to be "easy money." But she's going to learn that being a mom carries much, much more responsibility.

The Godfather: because there was a near-fatal attempt on Michael's father's life and now he learns it's difficult to resist inheriting the legacy of his family's criminal empire. He learns he has no choice.

In *Get Him to the Greek* our hero gets his dream: to hang out with his rock idol, but this becomes a nightmare when he learns that his idol is a manipulative, infantile, selfish drug addict. Aaron Green makes this choice fully expecting to live his fantasy of being friends with Aldous Snow. Oh boy — has he got another think coming!

In each of these, a shattering or forceful event — one that the protagonist has unintentionally caused — forces him/her to take the journey.

Why?

Because today is a day that promises change.

This "Why Now?" is the most important moment in conceiving your screen story.

Simply because your character "wants to be better" he chooses to go to school. YAWN.

Or your character hears that there's money to be made on Wall Street. YAWN-YAWN.

Or your character "thinks it might be cool" to do something (MAJOR QUINTUPLE YAWN!).

None of these qualify as "why now?" Your "why now?" must be part of the essential emotional platform of your movie.

"Because *today* this protagonist must be placed on a journey in which he/she gains understanding, chooses to change, or recognizes that his/her traits are flawed."

That's how "Why Now?" works and without it you cannot start your story.

Life Is Chaos. Movies Make Sense.

Why is that if you saw a huge spaceship descending into your neighborhood, you would probably call the police or the army or just run for cover? Alien spaceships. That doesn't make sense! And calling in the emergency is a pretty sensible thing to do.

Yet, in *Close Encounters of the Third Kind* an entire secret initiative of intelligence and the military is organized to meet these alien visitors and even our main character finds his brain invaded by images and impulses that bring him to the secret landing location. Makes perfect sense to me and, I'm sure, to you because it made perfect sense to millions of moviegoers who made this one of the biggest grossing box-office hits of all time. Nobody sat there and said, "Well that's not a sensible thing to do." But I'm certain we all took the leap of faith and believed it made sense.

When Robert Redford uncovers a rogue operation within the CIA, why doesn't he just phone it in? What's the big deal? If you saw somebody at your workplace doing something improper, wouldn't you just try to reason with them or help your workmates put a stop to it? Sure!

But not in a movie. And the last thing you want is someone *not* opening a door they shouldn't or just calling 911 or going into couples counseling and coming clean about infidelities. Makes for a pretty dull story.

That's because the behavior we expect in life is "sensible" while the behavior we expect in movies must "makes sense." This "sense" is based upon the inner and exclusive logic that is accepted by an audience (and the characters!) in order for us to surrender to the experience of the story.

Let's make some sensible choices for some of our favorite movies.

In *Star Wars: The Empire Strikes Back* Luke Skywalker must, once again, save the Federation (why can't they find someone with more experience?). So he is chosen to face off against the most powerful evil in the universe, Darth Vader (why don't they just blow up Vader instead of sending one fresh-faced kid?). And when Luke is almost defeated in hand-to-hand combat with Vader, he loses his hand, only to find out that Vader is the father he's missed all of his life. He's still able to do the right thing: refuse to cross over to the other side. He's willing to sacrifice everything to save the Federation.

In the world of the Jedi, the Empire v. the Federation, Yoda and Obi Wan Kenobi, it all makes perfect sense. Yet none of the choices could ever be called "sensible" in real life.

But a dramatic story isn't about your characters making sensible choices. Because *Star Wars* is fundamentally a coming-of-age story, the choices made by an impetuous youth, in a hurry to become a hero, make perfect sense.

In life, we make sensible choices: grow up, go to college, choose a career, have a family, and settle into a nice comfortable life, avoiding as many difficulties as possible.

That would be a remarkably boring movie.

It's when this "sensible-ness" is disrupted — and as early as possible in your story — that things get interesting, entertaining, and enlightening.

Your story is about this disruption. Your story allows the audience to appreciate the simple beauty of being sensible by watching other characters struggling with a dramatic lack of common sense.

Yet, if you threw in common sense, your story wouldn't matter, but your struggle as a writer is to make sure that your story makes sense. Seems like some kind of intellectual paradox.

There is no drama (or comedy) in being sensible. That's everyday life. Our "being sensible" is the only antidote we have to the senseless chaos of life. Life is not an organized affair, which is why we struggle as a civilization to bring some order to it. Life doesn't really make sense. You can be a perfectly nice person and still be the victim of an earthquake or a car accident.

So the only way we can try to make sense of it all is to produce science, art, and philosophy. Storytelling is one of our primary tools in bringing some sense to this senseless proposition. Storytelling organizes our thinking about each other and ourselves.

Your story's lesson to your protagonist is a lesson that we all need to learn, through the experience of your main character. Therefore, within your completely made-up story, there must be an order and structure to the life-like events that occur.

So when all of Robert Redford's colleagues are murdered while he's out getting lunch, it really doesn't make any sense in our real-life view. But in the view of the underbelly of this fictional world of spies, it makes more sense than anything in real life!

There's something else paradoxical involved.

Let's remember that even if we're creating so-called "real-life" events, the work is fiction. Even *Lincoln* is a fictional movie based upon strenuously researched facts. Let's face something: regardless of the "fact" that it might depict "actual historical events," they have been construed, contrived, and reinvented as screen entertainment.

We get something very important from this fictive experience: the truth about some great human value.

Strange, but we create an inner logic of an illogical story that makes complete sense, but is not sensible, which is a lie that tells the truth.

You got that?

As a writer you are lying. You are preaching some kind of life-lesson-type propaganda in order to share with your audience (and your main character) some great truth about life. I love this paradox and it allows a human value to dominate your story.

While we struggle in life to create a path for ourselves, it's really a tremendous achievement, not a given. When we avoid anxiety and conflict, that's considered living a "good life."

But not for your screen story.

When you are creating the world and journey of your character you will need to a) know that world either through personal experience or diligent research and b) create a sequence of cause-and-effect that constructs a logical path for your character's journey. This journey *forces* your character to make increasingly important and illogical (as in normal life) choices, which gives the experience excitement and anticipation for an audience.

So tattoo this to your brain:

- Life needs to be sensible, but only occasionally makes sense.
- Movies must make sense, but almost never show what's sensible.

The Promise: You get to keep every stupid, crazy thing you think up — but you must make it work!

I look forward to the moment when I put my work into the hands of actors and directors and they say to me, "I don't believe this moment" or "How do we get there from here?"

The basic problem is this: they know they must reach these moments and decisions through the actions of the character.

So many movies try to get there through the "suggestion" or "urging" of another character. Drama is not based on "word of mouth." Nobody told Michael Corleone it would be a good idea to become the next Godfather. Those three guys in *The Hangover* didn't simply hear that they should find their best friend and get him to his wedding. Was Spartacus (in *Spartacus*) told by another slave, "This ain't right, man. Somebody's gotta take a stand!"? The verbal urging of a character can only be believable under certain story conditions such as if someone hijacks his ship, or literally puts a gun to his head, or a terrorist is holding his daughter hostage, or makes him an "offer he can't refuse." These are coercive conditions that compel the character to put things right.

So you get to keep it all, provided you make the thing work in a believable way that makes sense in the world of your story.

Story Value: What's It Worth?

Your first step in story clarity is to create what I call an *action structure* document.

While I don't think it's a good idea to start with the human value of your story, it is part of structuring your story before you write your script. This document will help you figure it out.

So let's say you want to do a bank robbery movie. I think it's good to know your genre. Also, it's good to pick something that stimulates you enough to keep at it. You'll be writing this project for a few months at least.

In this bank robbery movie your hero has one last chance to get out of his criminal life and make a new life with his neighborhood girl.

So let's start with this guy. (This is based on the storylines of *Thief* and *Heat,* (both directed by Michael Mann) which have many similarities.)

This guy's been a bank robber for as long as he was able to hold a bag of money. His older brother was a bank robber, who was killed. Recently, he's met a woman he really cares about, but how is he going to have a life and be a bank robber? But now ("why now?") the head of the local crime syndicate is leaning on him to knock over a little bank outside of the city.

Here you have your character's major problems:

a) He's a bank robber. That's not a good thing! But it's all he knows. His life isn't fulfilled because of this and it causes lots of personal problems. Now he's in love and as great as that can be, that's also a problem because it's in direct conflict with his life and profession.

b) The crime boss is forcing him into another (he hopes, final) robbery job.

He's not a complete jerk or idiot. He really doesn't want to be a bank robber anymore. He wants a normal life. Something he's never known. But a) he has no other source of money and he needs money to change his life, and b) if he doesn't do it, the crime lord will kill him. So your first act is easy:

The following sets up:

a) The character and his problem, b) the Path to Satisfaction, c) the inciting incident, and d) the Call to Action.

ACT I

1. Jack, a talented career bank robber, wants to change his life and start a new one with his lady love, Karen. He asks her to marry him, but she says he's got to change his life or she won't say yes. (a, b, and c)
2. The local crime lord, Ozzie, drafts Jack to do a robbery in a small town. Even though Jack doesn't want to, HE MUST DO IT (my caps!). So Jack sets about to get his crew together and plan the robbery. He's convinced that this is his last run. He'll get the money and run away with Karen. (d)

His problem: he's always been a criminal and now it's going to be hell to get out of this world.

Path to Satisfaction: to rob the bank and get away with the money and run off with Karen.

But you, the writer (and the story), will teach him a lesson that will last. So here comes the lesson . . .

ACT II

3. Jack gathers his old crew and starts the meticulous plan to rob the bank. Meanwhile, Ozzie the crime lord is putting time pressures on Jack. Turns out Ozzie needs the money to resolve his own difficulties with even bigger crime lords who are leaning on him. There's also an FBI agent starting to get

suspicious and is on both of their tails. And Karen doesn't like this one bit! She's threatening to break the engagement and say farewell. Jack's in a real mess.

4. This mess continues and escalates (you'll figure out the specifics in another document, your *beat sheet*). But let it suffice to say that Ozzie pushes the robbery up too early. The FBI agent is closing in having busted one of Jack's crew. And Karen is packing her bags. Jack is screwed! All is lost!

ACT III

5. Now Jack MUST go through with the robbery. Of course, what can go wrong does goes wrong. And when Jack finds out that Ozzie ratted him out to the FBI, he goes and puts a bullet in Ozzie's head.

6. In the final chase, he's arrested and put on trial for murder. Jack now understands that the only way to get out of "the life" is to just get out while the getting is good, not to make a deal with the devil and expect to switch to the "good life."

And then you'll address your two big statements:

> **The active question:** "Will Jack rob the bank and get away with it?"
> **The story value:** "You can't make a better life by continuing your bad life."

This is a pretty loosely ad-libbed story just to show how you construct this little document. It will be no longer than one page, but it's got everything you need to pitch your story to other people (and build your confidence in it), and it also gives you an overview — a map — of the whole thing. One of the rare times going forward that you'll be able to see the story as one thing, the way an audience sees it (and yes, the way you see the face of a watch!). Notice a few other qualities:

- The ending *has a lot to do* with the beginning.
- The main character's choices *are the story*. His actions are what we are watching and experiencing. What he *does* — not what he *wants* — makes the story go where it goes.
- For most intents and purposes, your story appears believable in the world in which it is set. A journey back and forth in time is no less believable than a bank robbery. But they both have an inner illogic that rings true for the audience.
- There is a clear cause-and-effect that moves the story to its ending. (Notice I didn't use the word *forward*. Some stories don't exactly move "forward." They can move, intellectually, in many different directions. But one thing is certain: all stories have an end — yes, including prequels.)
- The main character is constantly under pressure. This pressure builds throughout the story until it explodes.
- The ending is surprising, yet inevitable.
- The story makes its own sense. We started out with a guy going through this particular struggle and we ended with a guy who got some kind of lesson from the struggle.
- What happened in between took us "through the world" of the journey. Even though he was familiar with it, it was new because of the pressurized circumstances.

I strongly believe these to be the rudimentary properties of a cohesive dramatic story (this also holds true for comedy). I also believe that only a very few films of any quality fail to adhere to these requirements and still prove successful with their audiences. In fact, if we want to easily learn the accepted patterns of dramatic construction, simply look at the masterpieces of animation from Disney and Pixar.

All of these stories are very disciplined in sticking to the rules. The primary reason for this is that young people, especially children, really don't enjoy unstructured entertainments. Kids want to know where they are in a story and conventional story structure is what tells an audience where they are in any story. Movies such as *Snow White*, *Toy Story*, and *The Iron Giant* are very conventionally structured and moderately executed stories that keep an audience interested simply by properly orienting them throughout the journey of our hero.

From here on in, you will be working with your "bricks," the pile of stuff that will be carefully assembled and connected to make your story.

The "Action Structure" of Your Story

This document will allow you to fully express the major story events and story value clearly and concisely. Not only good for getting started, this can also become the basis for your pitch or any other verbal presentation of your story, even in conversation. What it will force you to do is think about the value of your story before you write it. In that way, you will have a much more thoughtful approach to the storytelling process. This is the equivalent of an architect's initial drawings. This is equal to a conceptualization of the whole project before the actual detailed engineering.

- Ideally, it should be no more than one page.
- Try to fit it into six to eight paragraphs. Don't go into too much detail. Just write the major points.
- Write it in prose. Don't treat it like a form. It's about the emotional and dramatic value of your story.

You will divide it like this:

ACT I

1. Character and Setting

Know the backstory and character deficit of your protagonist. Distill it to a short phrase, like "A guy who always needs to prove himself." This inner flaw will be used as a constant source of conflict; a trait that always screws up your protagonist. It will also define the current reality and the world that your character is in at the start of your story. It will be this character's "path to satisfaction."

Examples: The world of *The Godfather* is the mafia circa 1940s to 1950s + Michael does *not* want to go into the family business; *Chinatown*, the life of a private detective in 1937 Los Angeles + a guy who's always cut corners, taken the "easy way"; *The Hangover*, a road trip through the southwestern US with three screw-ups trying to find their friend.

2. The Inciting Incident and Call to Action

The *inciting incident* brings the character in touch with the start of the story and believably leads to the *call to action*.

> **Inciting Incident:** It's something normal or everyday, but it must be done and is driven by the reality of the character's current circumstances.

Examples: "It's his turn to go get lunch" (*Three Days of the Condor*) or "he goes to a job interview" (*Being John Malkovich*) or "he picks up the wrong suitcase at the airport"(*What's Up Doc?*). Michael comes home from the war to attend his brother's wedding to introduce his fiancée to his family (*The Godfather*); Jake Gittes signs up the "phony" Mrs. Mulwray. That's his job. The three *Hangover* friends are invited to their friend's wedding. It's their best friend and they are the groom's ushers and best man.

Call to Action: The character must make a decision to go where he/she has never gone before. It's *not voluntary*. It's not a healthy response to their need for self-improvement.

DON'T: "Hey — I'm going to read this book on screenwriting! This will solve all of my problems!"

DO: "Hey — I better read this book on screenwriting or this kidnapper is going to shoot my mom!"

Examples: Michael Corleone must take action to protect his father at the hospital; Jake Gittes must take action against the people who tried to cut off his nose; The Buddies (*The Hangover*) must find their friend and figure out what the heck happened last night — who wouldn't?

> ### Tip
>
> This call to action will necessarily be opposed to their path to satisfaction. Michael Corleone still expects to be a legitimate citizen; Jake Gittes is absolutely convinced he can bring down Noah Cross; the Three Buddies simply have to find their friend and everything will be all right.

ACT II

3. The Journey: the Unfamiliar World; Further Complications and New Relationships

For the purposes of your action structure document, you don't need to furnish details about Act II. Don't worry, that comes later, with your beat sheet. Suffice to say that you understand that:

a) The character now finds his world turned upside-down and . . .

b) He encounters characters along the way who are either brand-new or, if familiar, are with him or against him.

Whatever happens, everything jeopardizes the main character's goal.

4. Squeezed into a Corner

This choice/obstacle makes it nearly impossible for the character to move ahead unless a major choice is made.

Your character is "on the ropes." It appears that this is all going to end very badly. "All is lost!"

What's the worst that can happen? *That's* what happens.

ACT III

5. The character is confronted by the worst possible circumstances; the greatest fears are realized: climax!

The climax occurs when the character ceases to struggle with the plot problem or ends his/her quest for satisfaction. In *Godfather*, it's when he kills off the heads of the other families. Yes, he's become head of the crime "family," but what about his *real* family? In *Midnight Cowboy* it's when Joe Buck nearly kills one of his older male "clients." He's finally seen the real side of being a male prostitute, but now something more important awaits his final attention: friendship.

6. The final choice is made, causing change or recognition.

- Joe Buck takes Ratso to Florida, the land of their dreams . . .
- Michael Corleone becomes the godfather and shuts out his wife.
- *The Hangover* Buddies find their friend, but soon learn the more important value of friendship versus "buddy-ship."

Then answer these questions:

- What is your character's path to satisfaction?

In the end,

- What does your character recognize about him-/herself?

- What has changed in the character's life at the end of the story?

ACTION STRUCTURE: *THE GODFATHER*

ACT I: *The World of the Character*
- Michael Corleone, a young marine, attends his sister's wedding. He vows to his girlfriend that he will not become like his father, Don Vito Corleone, or be involved in his kind of business. He loves his family, but wants a legitimate life apart from their criminal activities.
- One day, his father is shot and is near death. Michael must help to save his life. While guarding his father, he is punched in the face by a police captain. He is now drawn into the world of his father and his brother.

ACT II: *The Journey and the Ordeal*
- Michael becomes an assassin when he volunteers to kill the corrupt police captain and the son of another mafia leader. He hides out in Sicily, engaged to a beautiful Italian girl who is killed by local rivals. Back in the US, his brother Sonny is killed. He returns to the US, now angry and embittered, to take his brother's place alongside his father. (NOTE: all of the trouble above is caused by his choice to become a killer.)
- As time progresses, Michael takes on more and more of the responsibilities of Godfather and head of the family's criminal enterprises. Michael proves himself over and over as a capable warrior in the cause of revenge for the attempt on his father's life. He emerges as a gifted and innovative strategist in the growing gang war. His father makes a truce with the other families and also compromises his principles about being in the drug trade. Don Corleone dies.

ACT III: *Resolution*

- On a single day, Michael consolidates his power by assassinating the heads of the rival crime families and killing any others who have betrayed him. Michael resolves to be the Godfather, regardless of how his wife feels about it.

Path to Satisfaction: To have a legitimate life apart from his powerful family's criminal activities.

Change or Recognition: A "family" is a powerful force in life. Nobody can escape his/her family, but no one can escape the bonds of succession in a hierarchy like a crime family.

Chapter 3

....

SO THERE'S THIS PERSON . . .

You're Writing for Actors!

> "The sole task of the dramatist is to write great roles
> for great actors." —George Bernard Shaw

Here's a good question: once a script is accepted, who is largely responsible for a movie getting that "green light"? Yes, certainly the studio or network exec or the person with the money, okay, but . . . they still need a director and a crew — and even then, that green light is still meaningless. Nothing moves forward. And don't forget, you've got your teamsters and their trucks. But still, something's missing. You still ain't got no movie.

Actors! Specifically stars are the key element in moving forward with a production. In fact, you can have your stars lined up without the other elements and, as you probably already know, you can raise all of your funds based on their participation ("attachment") to your project.

Hollywood is fundamentally held hostage (in a good way) by these actors. It's just an accepted way of doing business. It's not corrupt, it simply reflects the importance of actors to the filmmaking process. Not only is it impossible to make a movie without them, an audience's perception of a film is firmly grounded on who is in it, and maybe also the genre and possibly the story.

But while this causes producers to break pencils and gnash their teeth, it also helps them gauge their prospects for a successful movie. That's because most of the time moviegoers aren't really interested in stories so much as they are in stars, although a big star in an uninteresting story doesn't work either. We've seen a lot of examples of that in movie history.

It's the stars. That's what people want to see. And stars, as they say in astronomy, are the sources of all light and all energy at the center of the system. That's the science of it.

So what's the big deal with creating a good script with a compelling story? Very simply: because actors want to be in that movie; that movie with the great role, with the wonderful story, where they get to act gallantly heroic, horribly bad, or terribly funny. They dream of *that* role. But it hasn't been written yet, except: you get to write them *that* role.

We see it all the time. What's Al Pacino doing in that low-budget Sundance movie? How did Steve Buscemi get to be such a big star? How did Brad Pitt go from being a teen idol pretty boy to being one of the most successful stars in the world? And what makes us go see *any* movie with Cate Blanchett (at least I do!)?

It might seem mystical to you, but my theory is pretty simple. Actors really know quality. After all, they are the last ones to handle it. It's their faces up there, enlarged to 60 feet x 40 feet. It's *their* movie, isn't it? This is the way most moviegoers usually talk about movies (I actually know a few people who are not in the movie business!).

"Y'seen that new Nicole Kidman movie?"

"Haven't seen it yet. But I went to that new Clooney picture. Not bad."

"I was curious about that, but I'm more interested in that Matt Damon movie."

. . . And not a word about Fincher, Scorcese, or Soderbergh.

While actors struggle like everyone else to be able to identify a winning script, they will be able to tell fairly easily what a good part is. That's because they don't look at how much money it might make or lose. They don't even care how much it might cost. For the most part, these wonderfully gifted people really want to act. Carpenters like to hammer, surgeons like to cut, and actors want to act.

They want to act like they've never acted before. They want to work as hard as they can to get that amazing performance in that great role, so they can win an Oscar. So they can be beloved worldwide. So they can get more chances to act in more great roles . . . and on and on.

This is because actors love to act. They are among the most hardworking artists in the profession. When they get a chance to do something great, they try to do something great. I believe it's one of the last truly magical processes left in movies. You really can't duplicate it electronically. A human being experiencing extreme emotions right in front of our very eyes is really an amazing bit of magic.

It's your job to give them that great thing to do. Can you think of a simpler formula for success as a writer? True, it's never that simple.

So here's an answer to our opening question: Since film is not completely a "visual" medium, what is it?

Film is a *performance medium.*

Actors are the key deciders in the fate of any film. If you don't have enough money for Brad, you'd be surprised at his willingness to do your movie anyway because it's such a great role (*Snatch*). Or inexplicably, an actress like Cate Blanchett goes from playing the title role as Queen Elizabeth, to a supporting role in *The Talented Mr. Ripley*. And George Clooney is not the star of *Gravity*. And how is it that Cher always seems to know exactly what role to take (one Oscar win, one nomination, and a slew of Golden Globes, and we're only looking at her dramatic movie and TV career, not counting her TV variety career with Sonny Bono).

I asked a friend who had worked with her how this could be and he said, "Cher knows what's good for Cher." So let's say a blessing for the self-centered professional nature of certain gifted actors. When it comes to making selfish choices, I'll bet they do better than most studio and network folks.

I don't think actors have a better "crap-detector" than anyone else. We all struggle with it. Sometimes our eyes bug out in amazement when we see a really terrific actor in something wholly abysmal. But that's another book. The circumstances that can sometimes put a certain actor in a certain movie are oftentimes simply bizarre and, just as often, the product of a process that leads to thousands of bad choices in filmmaking.

But Paul Giamatti does pretty well. So does Johnny Depp. And of course, Kate Winslet. For the most part, they tend to go for some pretty substantial stuff. And when they don't go for that, they probably take something that pays enough to give them the time to wait for that great role to come along.

Then there's Nicole Kidman. Unmistakably a perfectly marvelous actress who seems to never stop working. She really *likes* what she does.

She's done every type of film there is to do from the big-budget historical romance of *Cold Mountain* to the low budget "art" film *Fur* (with Robert Downey Jr.) to the enigmatic and avant-garde *Dogville* by Danish "dogma" director Lars van Trier.

This is an actress who loves what she does and wants to take herself to the limit as an artist. That requires courage, passion, and a profound love of what one does.

That's where you come in.

Actors have been students of drama and the art of storytelling for much of their careers. Even if they can't articulate it, their instincts are normally 100% correct for what gets them excited as artists. They're looking for an emotional range, something different and challenging, and a role that is uplifting for their artistic soul. There's this myth that actors are "phonies," or not genuine in their behavior. Most of us experience actors on the red carpet or on talk shows. In fact, due to their training, good actors have a unique relationship to their inner emotional life. When it comes to their work, they are about as down-to-earth and discerning as a master jeweler looking at a "fugazy" (see: *Donnie Brasco*).

Case in point. Here's something I heard about Wes Anderson and his breakout movie, *Rushmore*.

Wes had a quirky little script. But he needed a star. He was able to get the script to Bill Murray (I don't know how. That's another book.) and Murray rejected it, but with some suggestions as to how to improve it. Anderson complied and re-sent the script. Now Murray liked it a bit more, but still turned it down, albeit with a few more notes for improvements. Anderson complied yet again and after a few more passes that was that. Murray was on board and the rest, as we say, is history. Anderson's and Murray's working relationship helped to enhance both of their careers. This is not only a story of tenacity and self-producing, but also how to take notes and rewrite!

So in a world where "nobody knows anything . . . " it's actually true that actors might be the first line of defense in understanding what a good script may be. And yes, sometimes they are wrong in judging a whole screenplay. But build a good role and they will come.

Your Main Character Moves in Two Opposite Directions At Once

So who is this person? Your main character needs to be stupidly smart, brilliantly idiotic, righteously wrong, skillfully inept, sweetly insensitive, and indifferently loving.

Remember, your characters are all works of art. I don't mean they are sculptures and paintings. I mean they are a creation of your imagination but appear to have all the traits and behavior of real people. Even if it's a fish, a lion, or a cyborg, your characters are going to behave like human beings. In fact, they are going to be more than human. This doesn't mean "superhuman." It's more like "hyper-human." If they're bad, they're evil. If they're good, they're heroes. It's an exaggerated version of our everyday lives.

Your characters' humanity is going to be on display for very particular reasons.

This is why I always recommend that you start all story thinking with your main character.

What's in your action structure document? What's your character's big problem? Many people have referred to this as their "fatal flaw." I'm not a fan of the term. That always implied tragedy or death and we want to make sure that even if we are writing a tragedy, this problem isn't so much fatal as it is both the *motivating* as well the *resolving* factor in the life of your character within your story.

In *Casablanca,* Rick not only won't stick his neck out for anybody, he finally does and saves the Western world. Now that's screenwriting!

I have created the term *character deficit.* Like a bad debt, it has to be paid off and your story is the debt consolidation plan.

In *Maria Full of Grace,* Maria is a headstrong, stubborn seventeen-year-old. Every scene in Act I shows her either defying someone or insisting on her own way. This personality trait causes her to quit her job (the inciting incident). In the tiny Colombian town she lives in that's like a death wish. She goes on to defy her family and lie to them about her future prospects. She even shuns her boyfriend, the father of her unborn child who is more than willing to step up and marry her. But that's not good enough for our Maria! Nope! She's got to have it her way.

See how screenwriter Joshua Marston has this character push herself into a corner? Her character traits — her deficits — are driving her to a kind of psychic bankruptcy, so she is now spiritually and materially desperate.

Her hunger for independence and autonomy bring her face-to-face with a local "mule" recruiter. A guy who combs the country towns looking for young women just like Maria — and bingo, she goes for it.

Now her hardheadedness comes in handy. She's going to swallow about sixty heroin-filled condoms and import them in her belly to the US. When she and her best friend arrive, their only mentor dies. This leads Maria on a wild two days in Queens, lying again in order to stay with the dead girl's sister, and finally using her wiles to defend herself against the guys she hands off the drugs to. And guess what? She still manages to collect the money! Remember: she's tough!

Throughout this entire journey, Maria is never anything except stubborn, headstrong, and raging for independence, just like any other teenager. And every move she makes is completely believable. But this single character deficit leads her to make both bad and good decisions. This is good storytelling. It's great screenwriting.

The film, in my opinion, is a masterpiece of sober, well-structured filmmaking. But everything in the story is in service to and is caused by Maria.

Every moment revolves around her and what she's going to do next — whether it's initiating action, as when she escapes from her drug-dealer handlers, or when she decides to try to lie her way into a place to sleep. Each move is based on the overriding trait (a perfectly ordinary trait) that moves her through the whole journey.

All of the jams she gets into are a product of this teenage obstinacy. But the beauty of this story is that this bullheadedness is the very same thing that gets her out of her serial problems.

Her pregnancy and her rejection of the baby's father, the very elements that cause her to first quit her job and then to become a drug mule, is the condition that sets the story in motion. It's not a good thing to be an unwed pregnant teenager in a small town in Colombia. However, later, when she is detained at customs, carrying a few pounds of drugs in her belly, she is exempted from being X-rayed by US Customs. Why? Because she is pregnant!

Great Characters = Great Actors: Movies Are About Performance

So what do actors want from your script?

I think they want to be seen dealing with difficulty and adversity, getting into trouble, getting out of a jam or many jams, one after another. Whatever it is, it must be intense to be worth their efforts.

In *A Beautiful Mind* Russell Crowe's character can barely lead a normal life because of his deep mental illness. I'm sure that many stars were aching to do this character; they love this kind of problem-plagued personality. It lets them do what they love to do: act — and act big.

There's also a myth (but maybe not) that in a tight Academy Award race, "the one with the disease always wins." Now, maybe that doesn't actually happen every time (or does it?). But what people are really talking about is the strain of playing a handicapped or mentally ill character. Or as the Robert Downey Jr. character so bluntly puts it in *Tropic Thunder* "going full retard." (In this film, Downey plays a fully made-up black character, which was a pun on the entire concept of "full retard.")

You don't need to wonder why Oscar-winner Ben Kingsley took the role of brutal, irrepressible hit-man Don Logan in Jonathan Glazer's low-budget caper noir, *Sexy Beast*. It was about as great a role as his Gandhi and it showed his remarkable range as an actor. This is exactly the kind of juicy roles big stars look for to take their working vacations from mainstream acting.

Another good example is an obscure indie picture, *Buffalo 66*. In the opening fifteen minutes having just arrived via train to his hometown after being in prison, the only thing that Vincent Gallo (also writer and director) needs to do is find a place to pee. But he can't! It hurts just to watch this sequence. I'm sure when Gallo was creating the story he was saying to himself, "What can I do to keep this guy in a serious jam!"

Same for you: give your actors some intense and emotional material to do, to feel, and to say. Challenge them with a bumpy emotional ride, whether it's a thriller like *The Fugitive* or an internalized emotional journey like *The Ice Storm*. They'll want to do your script because they will want to go through that emotional experience.

This also helps actors feel they're growing as artists. Added to this, we all know that challenging roles with intense emotional peaks and riveting wrenching scenes get critics' and the public's attention. Every actor wants to be big onscreen.

But why do great actors appear in seemingly lousy movies? One reason is that there is a great role in there and in these cases, stars just want to do it.

A good example is Taylor Hackford's 1997 guilty pleasure classic *The Devil's Advocate*. I happen to adore this movie. Every role has a nice rich arc of action. Every character has his/her own beginning, middle, and end that adds up to a good amount of strong scenes for every performer, even in small roles. Every character has their one *big* scene. (See next section: "No Character Left Behind.")

But how does Al Pacino end up in a cult movie like this? Just look at the role he gets to play: Lucifer! Satan himself! The devil! And he gets this amazing, wild, crazy, eat-the-scenery monologue in the final scene.

That last monologue is like a six-minute Jimi Hendrix guitar solo. The role is irresistible.

Good writing — tight scene structure, conscientious storytelling, responsible screenwriting, and a good feel for a character's journey — will get you your star.

But no matter what the quality of the whole movie, you're more liable to tempt a star by writing a role that a great actor can sink some teeth into. Give your star a chance to win an Oscar. They'll love you for it.

No Character Left Behind

I've been a parent since 1991. I know what it's like to care for a child. I've also had aging parents in my life, so I know what it is to care for and worry about a loved one.

This may sound extreme, but it's the same way in screenwriting.

Your characters are your children; your loved ones. They need to be cared for, even if they're evil, careless, or stupid.

Characters are not people. They're fictional works of art based on humans. If they were actual people we wouldn't be able to represent them as deer (*Bambi*) or fish (*Finding Nemo*) or toys (*Toy Story*). The whole point is that we believe they are people, but they actually never existed. It's like a painted portrait. It's what the artist saw when he painted it, but it's not the actual person.

In a movie, as we work to engage our audience, we are made to care in some way about the characters. I want to avoid the idea of "liking" them. It's caring about a character that's important.

Caring about a character can mean being frightened of what they might do or sensing danger for our main character because he's made another foolish choice. Fearing an evil character is the same as "caring." A character needs to be made real and as writers this is our main task: create believable characters who demand our attention.

If we treated characters like people we would have very little respect for them or if they were our in-laws, we would ignore them and wish our time with them was over as soon as possible.

Characters in your story are functional objects in your story scheme, no different than eating utensils, but no less useful. That's the most formal way I can put it. Like chess pieces on the board, they are limited in function; however, they play a specific role in who wins and who loses and you must play the game with all of them.

More importantly, each character *does* something in your story that is meaningful. This may not include the bus driver or the news-stand guy. But if your main character interacts with them in some way, it must mean something and it must also be an important part of telling your story.

The three friends in *The Hangover* are a good example. These are not three of the same type of person. One is the handsome, confi-dent "leader" of the group (Bradley Cooper). Another is the straight-laced, touchy nerd (Ed Helms), and the other (Zach Galifianakis), a total loose cannon who can only be relied upon, in most cases, to refill the bong.

But the contrast of these three makes a stunning kind of energy machine come to life when the story hits the fan.

This is an example of conflict at the very moment your story begins. Here they are caught in a crisis and they must work together — quickly — to find a solution. But these three could no more cooperate on where to go to dinner let alone find an answer to why there's a tiger in their hotel room or how they got their hands on a Las Vegas cop car. There's no easy way this story is going to come out. It's going to be a struggle from beginning to end and all because these three characters are so different.

As each additional character appears, they will serve their own purpose in the progress of these misadventures.

Don't bring in an important character and then make him disappear. Even some of the least successful movies out there don't commit this unpardonable sin. You would no more abandon a character than you would your own child or a friend in distress.

In a more extreme analogy, it's the same (in my opinion) as using someone for money or sex or simple companionship just because you need it at that moment. You've had your way with this person and then you throw them out.

Like real people, your characters need to have a complete life. If you don't give them that life, then your audience will not care about them or respond to them in a significant way.

Each character in any screen story gets something out of the story. Like your protagonist, each one has an inciting incident, a call to action, a story goal, and a win/lose at the end of the story.

Yes, for the most part, it's your protagonist who goes through the greatest stress and struggle in your story. But the characters who become part of this story also have unique traits that are designed to cause a response in your character and move the story forward.

Chapter 4

WHY IS THIS STORY SO IMPORTANT FOR YOUR HERO?

SO WHY DID Maria need to go through a journey that caused her to get pregnant, quit her job, and become a drug mule? Because she needed to understand that there are more important things in life than herself. She's pregnant the entire time and in her own way Maria is going through this for her unborn child. Maria must learn something important from this journey or she will be doomed to repeat it. In the end, and in character, she makes a final courageous, hardheaded, and rash choice. But it is absolutely the right choice. (Remember: the ending is a surprise, but it is inevitable.)

By putting Maria through this ordeal and only *this* ordeal, she's learning a lesson that will last.

What was her path to satisfaction? Delivering the drugs and getting her money. She is successful. But even that doesn't go so well. There's death, a labyrinthine journey in a faraway place called New York City, and nobody in New York knows Queens! Then by the skin of her teeth and her own tenacity, she gets the money.

But even at that point in the story, she still has to resolve her life.

In finding this trait for your character it should be something that everybody needs help with.

In *Chinatown*, Jake Gittes is just too sure of himself and is distanced from his heart and soul. In the end, he gets a tragic lesson in venturing out into unfamiliar territory.

In *The Godfather*, Michael is deluded into thinking he can stay away from his family's business. But he never gets a chance to think. First his father is shot, then he kills for revenge, then his beautiful young wife is assassinated, and before he knows it, his fate as the godfather is sealed.

In *Rosemary's Baby*, Rosemary is innocent to her husband's ultimate evil. She soon learns that even the most innocent can be the most evil.

In *Gravity*, Ryan (Sandra Bullock) actually *never* thinks she's going to get out of this alive and deep down we believe, as she does, that she won't. Her belief isn't simply based on her natural fear. Who wouldn't be afraid? It's based on her lack of will. She doesn't actually believe there's much to live for. But how many of us have ever been in a situation where we look up at the mountain and think, "The hell with it. Dying is easier."

She proves to herself that this disaster is worth surviving and despite seemingly unbeatable odds, she understands that life is worth living and that survival is worth fighting for.

In these movies, it's easy to see how the character deficit plays out over and over again as the character is pulled into his/her story ever more deeply. This makes it simple to push your character forward, but also show them making the same mistake over and over.

In *Midnight Cowboy*, Joe Buck keeps trying, over and over, to become New York's most desirable male prostitute. What a numskull! But this is where the drama comes from. You can't bring Joe Buck face-to-face with the very thing he needs (friendship) until you've stripped him of his deficit. This happens at the end of Act II when Joe nearly murders his last client.

In *The Hangover*, these three idiots need to learn how important lasting friendship is. So even though it's fun to party, it's also dangerous. But if there were ever a trio that can be expected to trip on their own dicks, it's these guys. Each one, especially their "leader" (Bradley Cooper), is utterly underqualified to take on the challenges of their journey. Now that's funny!

In all of these examples, please note how underqualified the main characters are. Michael Corleone has never really been a gangster; Joe Buck could never be a male hooker; Maria is a flower factory worker, not a drug dealer; and our guys in *The Hangover* are supposed to be responsible friends out for a good time, but manage to push the envelope of disaster.

In each case, it is their basic character deficit that continues to generate the drama and comedy of the story.

The "Fatal Flaw"

This is an expression that has been used in writing and literature since ancient times. It's sometimes called the "tragic flaw." It is this quality in your character that will lead him/her into conflict. I like to think of it as your character's comfort level with his/her own outmoded system of solving problems and his/her struggle to maintain it at any cost. Just like you, your character has gotten used to doing things the same way; even if it doesn't really solve any problems, it's easy and familiar.

Things like being stuck in a dead-end job, a long engagement to the wrong person, putting up with your family's negativity and even eating at the same restaurant every Wednesday. These habits are actually bad habits in your story and they are about to be broken.

A more dramatic way of using the tragic/fatal flaw is by making it the energy that propels your character through the story.

In *Being John Malkovich* Craig thinks he really can control things as he would one of his stringed puppets. But he's going to be proven tragicomically wrong in the end.

Same with Michael Corleone. He is always saying (lying!) about how the Corleone family will someday be completely legitimate, which he might actually believe. But his fatal flaw is his natural determination to "take care of the family business." He can't help it.

In *Chinatown* Gittes has a very tragic history when it comes to women. But that's not his flaw. His flaw is that he doesn't recognize it. In the end he really must face what he's done.

The fatal/tragic flaw can be something that your main character will see and change, or as in Hamlet, it will be the trait that destroys his world and creates tragedy for the characters in your story.

Your Character Is Looking for Satisfaction — But You're Gonna Make Him/Her Sweat for It!

So we've been over this before, but this is the perfect place to look at it more closely. This "satisfaction" thing . . .

In every film story the audience's excitement seems to grow with each rising level of difficulty presented to the character. It's like a circus. You're watching this guy ascend this ladder, up, up, up about fifty feet and you're thinking, "Glad it's him and not me!" The miracle is: you actually would never do anything as crazy as this, yet it gets you excited to see someone else do it.

Good stories are similar. Except instead of defying gravity, the story is going to show your character defying being "sensible." That is, all the everyday rules of life are going to either rapidly or gradually just fall away. This battle between the "sensible" and the "path to satisfaction" is part of the energy of conflict that is always present in a good dramatic story.

In *Maria Full of Grace* all she needs is money for her family. So what does she do? Become a drug mule! So now her path to satisfaction is going to be to simply deliver the drugs, get the money and get back home, just as planned . . . right . . . ?

But in your story, this is the thing that's going to kick your protagonist's ass. Joe Buck is going to find out how stupid he is to try to become a male hustler. The three friends in *The Hangover* learn that simply having a great bachelor party is a very bad idea. Jake Gittes will find out that taking on the most powerful forces in Los Angeles is a recipe for tragedy.

However, in the end, they are better people. In the end they have gone through this ordeal to become better at life and to reach an understanding that had not been there before the story began. In the end they are going to see that they've been wrong about how to deal with life all along! But now things just might be different.

So now, as you begin to build your story, you should have:

- Your main character
- The character deficit
- The path to satisfaction v. the lesson. These two should be dramatically opposed.

The third should present enough basic opposition to keep your story in a constant state of conflict. Your character's decisions should be a constant struggle for him or her to get onto that path to satisfaction. He/she should never give in to "the lesson" — not until the very end.

In *Star Wars* Luke Skywalker simply wants to become a Jedi. But he is constantly beset by decisions that force him to be the savior of the Federation. Again, he's always struggling with himself. His character flaw is "he wants to train to be a hero"; the lesson is "it's not that easy. You've got to fight for yourself and humanity if you want to be any kind of hero."

In *Midnight Cowboy* Joe Buck never gives up trying to be a male hustler. It's the very thing that leads him to befriend Ratso Rizzo, and Joe is at first conned by him. But this also leads to what will become the bittersweet ending: he and Ratso become each other's only friend. All of Joe Buck's decisions, despite every single wrong turn he makes, are based on his pursuing his path to satisfaction.

In *Chinatown* Jake Gittes never once thinks he's headed for doom — and neither do we! Because Jake is trying to do something so heroic and so out of character for him, we root for him all the way. Even after he tells Evelyn about his toxic past. Even after his former colleagues warn him he's getting in over his head.

In the most telling and ironic moment in the film, Jake has been captured by one of his former beat partners Lou Escobar and another detective. He tricks them into thinking he's saying good-bye to Evelyn, but instead is able to escape and further aid Evelyn's final, fatal exit. Just as Jake leaves them, getting a break from his former pal by making up a story about his love affair with Mrs. Mulwray, Escobar says to him, "You never learn, do you, Jake?" To which Jake sarcastically answers, "I guess I never do" as he gives them the slip.

Master screenwriter Robert Towne has concocted an utterly ironic moment for our hero. He's actually giving himself the slip. As always, overconfidently ignoring the forces arrayed against him. No, he'll never learn. This is one of a handful of pieces of thematic dialogue that give this film its resonant values and makes it watchable over and over again.

While it's important to send your character at full speed toward a brick wall, what you are doing as a writer is offering them an alternative. It will not be to your hero's liking. He/she will feel uncomfortable choosing it, but in the end that's what your hero *must* choose.

These are the "value elements" in your story and with these, you can begin to build the events that will lead your character to a goal that should be almost the opposite of his/her path to satisfaction.

In *The Hangover* our guys simply want to enjoy a knockout bachelor party. But the story is going to teach them, "There's more to life than just getting drunk and partying with hookers." Their entire path to satisfaction is to get to a place of comfort (which is true for any protagonist). And their ordeal is like no other in this type of comedy story.

Another action comedy that should be mentioned here is Martin Brest's *Midnight Run* with a fantastic script by George Gallo. Here Robert De Niro plays a well-seasoned bail bondsman who's looking to get out of the game, but first, one last run to pull in the needed cash.

What is De Niro's character deficit? He's a bail bondsman! His very profession has led to all of his personal problems: his divorce, the fact that his wife hates him and hated her life with him, that he can't see his daughter, that he has ulcers. But also, that in his past, as a cop in Chicago, he tried to blow the whistle on corruption — and lost! He lost his ideals. Worst of all, he basically hates himself. Not a good state of mind to be in.

So, when we meet him, he's pretty desperate. He *must* take on the assignment of delivering the Charles Grodin character back to prison in order to get that money. It's a hilarious and heart-stopping cross-country chase. De Niro and Grodin are chased by the mob, the FBI, and competitive bail bondsmen. Added to this, these two guys can't stand each other, but later, save each other. Good conflicted storytelling.

Like *The Hangover*, *Midnight Run* depicts De Niro just wanting to get to the other side of his journey and deliver his fugitive. He's doing the job that he's done for decades; the job that has given him both success and misery. But the lesson is: "Nothing is easy, pal!" especially when you hate yourself. So, in this story the lesson is: "Live life as a happy person, not an unhappy person!"

In any film story with solid values as its core, this conflict between "satisfaction" and "story value" will generate the drama that the story needs.

Remember: You are writing your story because there is a conflict within the character that needs to be resolved and you are taking this character on the journey that will cause a drastic moment in his/her life that will necessarily cause a change in this person's coping mechanisms.

Your main character's conflict is the opposite of the theme. If the theme is "Crime doesn't pay," then he's a criminal. If the theme is "Don't tangle with evil," then the character thinks she can take care of a problem but learns she can't — or must triumph over an ultimate weakness to solve the problem.

Dramatic conflict is not simply an argument. It is a character struggling with goals that are huge and vital, and extends to the audience, who are moved to become involved in this struggle and care about your character.

"If It Weren't for Me, Everything Would Be Fine!"

Finally, I get to talk about Oedipus again. What's his character deficit? He thought way too much of himself. The lesson: humility.

The Greeks loved their drama. Especially these tragedies because they dramatized in their stories the flawed nature of humanity and an individual's role in the course of destiny in a harsh universe. Yum!

Oedipus heard from an oracle (a fortune-teller elevated to priestly status) that he would murder his father and sleep with his mother. Nonsense, he thinks! That can't happen to *me*. I am Oedipus! So he leaves his hometown of Corinth for Thebes determined to trick fate.

On the way, he kills an older guy who won't let him pass on the road. He doesn't know who the guy is, but thinks little of it except that the guy was a pain.

He arrives in Thebes to learn that their king, Laius, has just been murdered. But right now they need someone to help them with the horrible Sphinx. If you can't answer his riddle, he eats you alive!

Oedipus answers the riddles, rids Thebes of the Sphinx, and becomes their king. He marries Laius' widow, Jocasta, and everything's fine, at least for a little while. This is just the kind of unhealthy self-reinforcement Oedipus really does not need.

Soon, Thebes is beset with plagues and famine. No crops, and all the women become barren. Another oracle, a blind prophet, tells them that all they have to do is find the man who killed Laius and everything will be fine again.

But now Oedipus has a creepy feeling about this guy he murdered on the road, even though witnesses have said that Laius was murdered by a band of five thieves. "And anyway," Jocasta reassures him, "oracles don't know what they're talking about. We had a son and an oracle told us that he would kill his father and sleep with his mother. It never happened, because we left this kid to die on the hillside, a needle through his ankles to make sure he couldn't survive."

Oedipus is *comforted* by his wife's words (my italics!). What kind of mother would do this!

Again, the path to satisfaction is that "Oracles are BS!" But the way things turn out, it's anything but true. Every oracle who opens his mouth in this play is always spot on. Poor bullheaded Oedipus — big hero! big king! — just won't face the truth. In fact, he has killed his father and now he's married to his real mother and everything he's done to avoid it has actually contributed to making sure it happens.

It's all explained in the play: He was the baby on the hillside. He was adopted by the king and queen of Corinth. He killed Laius — his real father — on the road and then went on to marry the man's widow, Jocasta, his real mother.

Wow. Are you beginning to see why audiences flocked to this drama for over a thousand years?

Every move that Oedipus makes brings him closer to the truth, yet he refuses to believe it because he's being reassured by those he trusts (Jocasta) and himself that everything's okay.

Not!

At every turn, Oedipus is testing the prophecy but bending the truth to suit his comfort zone. In a way, he's sick. But every protagonist must have a "pathology" similar to this. Protagonists just refuse to take the hint. So every move they make is simply wrong. Every time they make a decision it thrusts them deeper into their own character deficit.

They refuse to see the problem. And more importantly, they rely on old methods to try to solve their problem.

Finally, at the end, when Oedipus understands everything that has happened, he goes to murder Jocasta, but she's hanged herself.

So he borrows her jewelry to gouge out his own eyes. It's all he can do to bring himself back down to the truth of his life.

Throughout the entire story audiences are screaming to themselves: "Oedipus! Schmuck! Don't do it! Listen to the oracle! Don't defy the prophecy! Don't defy fate! That's just plain stupid!"

But he can't listen to anyone but himself.

So your protagonist is not just stubborn in this way, he or she is a downright bonehead.

They say in the world of addiction recovery that the only way addicts (like junkies or alcoholics) will make the choice to change their lives is when they have touched rock bottom. In life, we don't want this to happen. But in movies that's *exactly* what you want to happen. You want your protagonist to feel the absolute and merciless sting of the complete failure of his/her mission. Your protagonist's system of coping with his/her problems just plain sucks!

You want to take this character down as far as you can until he/she gets it . . . finally. Absolutely. Without doubt.

You do this in your story by orchestrating a series of desperately wrong choices that your protagonist makes over and over again.

The engine for these choices is the "satisfaction" (Oracles are wrong!) versus the "story value"(Fate is fate, pal, and there ain't no two ways about it).

In your story you're putting your protagonist through the laundry. You're washing, rinsing, spinning, drying, and folding this character until he/she finally lies, exhausted, ready to be worn (stupid analogy, but it works).

Your protagonist has walked into every bad punch in the face he/she can. And now it's time to face up to the fact that he/she was wrong all along or that if he/she tries he/she really can win or if he/she just learns how to love he/she can be loved.

The lesson, whether it's a comedy or a tragedy, is usually very important. So the choices your character makes will bounce him/her around like a pinball until he/she relents.

In *The Godfather*, everything Michael Corleone does is in service to what he believes will save his father's life. That's a good thing! But who his father really *is* (a crime boss) makes all of Michael's good deeds evil. All of the good he tries to do only brings evil upon himself. His actions result in the murder of his brother Sonny. He is directly responsible for the murder of his brother-in-law Carlo and ultimately, in *The Godfather Part II*, the murder of his own brother Fredo. All of his actions are justified as revenge stemming from the shooting of his father and further betrayals to his family. But they are all acts of evil. Just like Oedipus, the very thing he feared becoming is the very thing he becomes. That's why this is such a durable drama.

Your character will make every wrong decision possible in relation to the story value. Each of his/her actions must be based on his/her path to satisfaction. This inherent conflict between the two will bring real dramatic turmoil to your story.

Remember: the path to satisfaction is based solely on the protagonist's character deficit. If your protagonist takes repeated actions based upon this flaw, there will be continuous conflict in your story.

"Schmuck!" "Idiot!" — Nicknames for Your Protagonist

It's hard to be on your protagonist's side and also *not* be on your protagonist's side. Yes, your protagonist is a sympathetic creature. Someone who we need to "root for" or for whom we're making a commitment to for a short period of time — anywhere from one and a half to just over two hours. So it's important that we believe in the actions this character takes.

But drama needs to hold our interest, so it's very important your character does not come up with the solution to his/her problem too quickly. Otherwise, you run the risk of a one-minute movie with no drama.

So the choices that your character makes must prove him/her to be a little bit of a dumbbell. Your protagonist has minimal resistance into being sucked into the trouble that you have planned, but also must have the necessary skills to get out of it. It's a delicate line you walk as a screen storyteller. This character must be smart and stupid in alternating actions and beats of your story.

You must always be secretly laughing at your character's foolishness. You know from the start that your character's beliefs in his/her world will change — but the character does not know that. You're obligated to take your protagonist through every step of the ordeal of misfortune or he/she will not earn or gain the understanding needed to experience the big change or recognition at the end. In turn, the audience won't get anything out of it if you make it too easy. So the "sensible" choice is the dull choice. But how do you make the "story choice" make sense?

In *Bicycle Thieves* (US title: *The Bicycle Thief*) our hero, Antonio, has a very interesting character deficit: he's proud and believes that justice is deserved. He won't give in to the common beliefs of his world. He struggles against an entire city — Rome! — in order to learn a very difficult lesson: mercy. Yes, a wonderful idea to set your hero against not just another person but a whole city. So in this amazing story, Rome itself acts as a kind of antagonist.

In this masterpiece of irony, writer/director Vittorio De Sica takes our guy and his nine-year-old son on a journey through a city that becomes less and less familiar to our hero, even though it is his native town (see: *Three Days of the Condor*).

His path to satisfaction is simple: to recover his stolen bicycle, which he desperately needs to perform his new job. A job in this world is like a precious diamond.

But De Sica uses this to haunt his character with his own deficit: this irreconcilable pride and belief in civilized justice that drives him on and on until he himself psychically and spiritually collapses under the weight of it.

But let's look at the fundamental proposition of this monumental story. This character must get his bicycle back if he is going to perform the desperately needed job he's won. It's postwar Rome. The city (and Italy) are in impoverished chaos. A job is like finding a bag of money.

So when his bike is stolen, we feel his desperation. Of course, he goes to the cops. They're no help. Then he goes to a friend. This then leads him to a search of the entire city to find his bike.

Is he crazy?

Well, yes, a little bit. Just like Michael Corleone is a little crazy to assassinate a gang rival and the chief of police over dinner. Just like Jake Gittes is nuts to take on Noah Cross. Just as certifiably insane is Joe Buck for thinking he can go from Texas to New York City and become a successful male prostitute. Just as crazy as Craig Schwartz who believes he can live in John Malkovich's body and control him!

I mean, you gotta be nuts!

But imagine if they weren't?

Imagine if they did the sensible thing.

If Jake Gittes got his nose cut by two ruthless henchmen and decided, with all due common sense, that you shouldn't tangle with these killers.

Or the buddies in *The Hangover* decided, "So what if he's going to miss his wedding. It's not our problem, is it?"

Or if Antonio simply understood that it isn't practical to search the city for his stolen bike. He'll just have to buy another one or he'll have to get another job that doesn't require the use of one's own bicycle.

Oh well, that's that! Movie running time: fifteen minutes.

But then you wouldn't have a story. You wouldn't have drama. You wouldn't have a movie.

Your Protagonist's Character Deficit Must Coincide with His/Her Journey to Change.

Let's match up a few in this exercise.

EXERCISE Character Deficit and the Journey to Change

Choose five movies — please avoid superhero or action films — and describe the difference between the protagonist's character deficit and the lasting lesson he/she learns at the end of the story. Here are examples from the preceding chapter:

FILM TITLE	MAIN CHARACTER	CHARACTER DEFICIT	CHANGE
Chinatown	Jake Gittes	He's a "wiseguy"; thinks he's got it all figured out.	Crushed by opposing forces he never had the skills to deal with.
Maria Full of Grace	Maria	Self-involved young woman who thinks she can live independently in the world without consideration of others' needs.	She'll learn a hard and life-affirming lesson when she tries to do something that she has no business doing.
Midnight Cowboy	Joe Buck	A hick who thinks everything is going to go his way simply because he desires it.	Sees that simple friendship is probably the most valuable asset he can have.
Bicycle Thieves	Antonio Ricci	His pride and a conviction that his self-respect will bring him his rightful reward.	The world does not operate on as high a standard as his beliefs. His downfall is that he will be the beneficiary of real mercy — something he has not shown to the people he has encountered in his journey.
Oedipus	Oedipus	This young king makes a conscious decision to defy fate as well as the gods.	He's going to learn that fate is immutable and to defy it is the act of a deluded man.

EXERCISE   Character Bios

- Write a complete biography of each major character in your story. Answer these and any other questions you can create:
  - Where was he/she born?
  - What's his/her problem(s) in life?
  - What his/her big dream in life?
  - What was his/her relationship with his/her parents?
  - How did he/she do in school?
  - What do his/her friends think is great about him/her? . . . Not so great?
  - What's this person's "big secret"?
  - Add some of your own topics and ideas.

CHECKLIST   The Protagonist

The progonist is the character . . .

- ☐ who is least replaceable.
- ☐ with the strongest story purpose; who the story is about.
- ☐ whose POV shapes the story.
- ☐ who has the most screen time.
- ☐ whose need(s) dominates the story.
- ☐ who sets the story in motion.
- ☐ whose actions have the greatest consequence to others.
- ☐ with whom we identify most strongly.
- ☐ who is most changed at the end/who needs the most change.
- ☐ who makes the decisions that propel and guide the story.

Chapter 5

. . . .

IF YOU DON'T BELIEVE THIS
STORY, WHO WILL?

SINCE YOU'RE THE BOSS of this whole thing, here's a handy little keep-sake that will reinforce your stature as a writer:

$$\text{Auth-} \left\{ \begin{array}{l} \text{-or} \\ \text{-ority} \\ \text{-entic} \end{array} \right.$$

Believability is a very tricky thing in movies. We believe that Luke Skywalker can lift an X-wing fighter solely with the power of his mind. We also believe that Noah Cross (in *Chinatown*) has the absolute power to subvert the laws of Los Angeles and in the end get everything he wants. We also believe that a boy's toys have a complete life of their own when he's not looking (*Toy Story*).

But these seemingly hard-to-believe elements are based on a process in which the writer has built a sequence of actions that will logically or illogically lead to these outcomes and the audience will believe it. If a writer has done his homework, you will be on the edge of your seat because you're not even questioning the basis for such believability.

Earlier I stated that "movies are real" while live performances can seem artificial in comparison. This is because your audience arrives ready to believe. You job is not to let them down.

As a writer it's your obligation to the characters — yes, that's right, *not* the audience — to place them in a world that is both convincing and takes them from one action to the next with a working logic that serves your story.

You *Can* Make This Stuff Up!

How many screenwriters have or have had careers in law enforcement? How many screenwriters were actually Jedi Knights? How many screenwriters murdered a rapist and then (joyously!) drove a car off a cliff with their best gal friend? Finally, how many screenwriters have ever actually done or experienced any of the stuff they write about?

Right: none, or very, very few.

So what about this "write what you know" thing everybody is always talking about? It's still true. Because what you are actually writing about is the human value — which you are an expert on!

I never knew anything about gold mining in Indonesia. Now I'm an expert. How do I know what I know? Without proper research and/or great source adaptation material, your script will be, in a word, stupid. You have to be the expert on the world and the subject you're writing about, even if it's a romantic comedy. Your source: all of human experience!

I also know I'm an expert on gold mining in Indonesia because I wrote a script about it. It also involves the end of the Indonesian dictatorship of the 1990s. But I've never been to Indonesia, never worked a goldmine, and with the fluky exception of having taken a "Geology for Poets" class in college — solely to fulfill some academic requirements — I know nothing about geology.

But I looked stuff up. I trawled the Internet, read books, looked at old magazine and newspaper articles, and put together the history of the Canadian equivalent of the Bernie Madoff affair. It was known as the Bre-X gold scandal of 1996. I'd say that I spent a good five or six months doing only research, making notes, compiling a huge inventory of information.

Then I started my outline/beat sheet. Since this was based on a factual occurrence, I had a little help from the actual history. The time structure of my story was fundamentally lined up already, rather than the other way around.

It's not a bad script. It's had a dedicated producer/director attached to it for eight years. Although unproduced as of this date, we've had strong positive reactions and some deals that almost got it in front of the camera.

But the biggest compliment I got was after I'd finished a draft, I gave it to an independent producer friend. She's smart. Very picky. Liked the script, but couldn't do it — it's expensive! But she liked it enough to show to her husband who just happened to be a mineral rights attorney. That means he works with global mining companies all over the world on big mineral mining deals — gold, silver, tungsten, you name it. Indonesia is a big, big player in his world.

After doing me the great courtesy of reading my script, he asked his wife, "How long was this guy in the mining business in Indonesia?"

Of course this is the greatest compliment a screenwriter can get, at least for this kind of fact-based script. I carry that in my heart always and I will trot it out once in a while — like now — to show off a little bit.

However, more than showing off, it's to prove a point: you can't know too much about the world of your story. If you are not a complete expert on your world or your character's skills (like bank robbery, meth manufacturing, car theft, the law, medicine, etc.) you won't write a convincing story.

So many of my students walk into class with a pitch about a "hit man" or "drug dealer" or an "ex-con." I have to humor them because everyone has the universal right to write anything they desire.

But how many college students have been hit men, or drug dealers (hopefully not), or been in prison (and I don't mean for breaking a window or teenage shoplifting. Hey, it happens!)?

So while I would always caution them about writing on subjects that appear to be imitations of "grown-up" movies, I would also tell them, "It's okay if you want to do a script on a hit man. But what's the 'value' of the story for the character and how are you going to research the subject so that you're an authority on it?"

Most of these more exotic characters happen to come from fiction and other movies. So, be my guest, read and see everything on the subject and you'll have the foundation for writing about it authoritatively. But will you exceed the originality of your source material? It's unlikely.

Robert Towne did years of research unearthing the actual scandal that *Chinatown* is based upon. In fact, it's well known that the actual scandal took place around 1917 to 1920, not the late '30s. But his knowledge, his being a native of LA and having been a boy during the period of this story, combined with his sense of wanting to pay homage to the film noir detective stories of Raymond Chandler and Dashiell Hammett, led to the stylistic hybrid that made that movie a timeless masterpiece.

The reason I am both frightened and eager to start a new project is precisely this: like my character, I am about to enter a whole new world that I've never known. My life and craft is like being Alice and perpetually running down yet another, completely different rabbit hole and coming out the other end with an immense amount of new knowledge.

Write what you don't know — but learn everything about it you can!

You're also an expert on your own life. This is something I urge all my students to do. That is, to go back home and make the movie about where they are from. Or make a movie about an experience that changed your life. You will easily be the only expert on this story. But you still need to do the research that is required for that story. You're the expert or you're as ignorant as the audience.

EXERCISES

- Open up a newspaper. Find a good story. Research it. See if you can find the story value.
- Continue developing this story if you think it might make a good script.

Zombie Rules: Believing the Unbelievable

It's funny, when I ask anybody these questions . . .

- How do you calculate your income?
- How easy is it to contract bubonic plague?
- When did World War I begin?

. . . there's usually a long pause even among the best educated.

However, simply ask *anybody* how to kill a zombie and the answer will fly out faster than you can say "zombie": "You cut off his head!" Same thing happens when you ask somebody how to kill a vampire: "Drive a stake through his heart while he's still sleeping in his coffin." How do you kill a werewolf? "Shoot him with a silver bullet." These questions never fail to produce the same answer as swiftly as a silver bullet travels.

It just goes to prove that audiences will believe anything as long as you provide some kind of foundation that makes enough sense. But then again, you try to make people believe that the CIA funded a clandestine operation to plant explosives in Fidel Castro's cigars and they'll say, "No way!"

But it's true!

Many screenwriters call this a screen story's *inner logic* or *inner illogic* as the case may be. I prefer to call it *Zombie Rules*. Much more fun. Much more movie-like. It's because these so-called "rules" come from fiction, not fact.

I paraphrase, but it was Mark Twain who inspired many screenwriters to proclaim: "Never let a few facts stand in the way of a good story."

I believe that one does not force an audience to believe the unbelievable. I like to think that as storytellers we allow the audience to believe the hard-to-believe. We open the door, as it were, to their probable belief in something that may not be very believable, but in the context of good storytelling, an audience will force themselves to believe it. You just need to know how to present it.

Looper is one of the very good examples. We all know the rules of time travel, don't we? (Better, I'm afraid, then we know the rules of driving on a highway!) The "rule" states that if you move ahead or back in time that the alteration of any event or object will necessarily result in a kind "event echo" (like the circles in a puddle) that will alter all events forever. It's the pesky "butterfly effect." Scientific fact, right? No — Zombie Rules!

However, try to make a time travel movie without acknowledging this rule and you'll have a difficult time convincing your audience of anything. Wasn't there a movie called *The Butterfly Effect*?

Looper takes this concept quite a few steps further. It proposes that in the near future assassins will ultimately be their own targets, depending on the time frame and the demands of criminal enterprises (the only ones who perform this illegal time travel from a future time).

Looper accomplishes its Zombie Rules by showing how convinced the characters are about the actual rules. Once an audience sees that the characters understand and obey the rules, they will go along with it.

Another way to put some strong Zombie Rules in your story is to use a character (your protagonist if possible) who is unfamiliar with these rules. The process of initiation and the learning curve is shared with the audience. But don't be a story klutz. When you do this, don't simply have these rules explained. Try to come up with sequences and scenes where your characters learn firsthand, i.e., by their mistakes and actions. Get them into trouble! This way the process becomes part of your story and part of the drama of your character's journey.

Chapter 6

....

SUSTAINABLE SCREENWRITING

The Story Is *Always* Being Told

So what's your contribution to this "energy" machine?

Something that I see with my students and even seasoned screenwriters — including me — is that we may at times allow our story to just languish; the energy flags; things slow down.

Sure, over time any energy-generating machine may need to slow down, conserve, and even stop in order to properly manage its energy. But stories must necessarily be different.

This energy slowdown frequently happens during Act II. The reasons for this are multiple. There may simply be a fundamental loss of imagination. We run out of ideas with which to challenge our hero and so simply allow the "placeholder" effect to occur. We lay in a scene or sequence we know is weak promising to replace it with something stronger later in the process. But somehow that stronger material just never appears.

Let's remind ourselves that all stories are based on *action*. I don't simply mean a car chase or a bunch of explosions and stunts. Action is what the main character *does* to continue moving toward the goal. Action is comprised of the responses of the main character to the obstacles that you put in the way.

Given the path to satisfaction and your ability to throw more obstacles in the path, this should create enough turmoil to keep you and your character busy for about 60-80 pages (depending on the total length of your script).

Here are a few things to keep in mind as you get bogged down in Act II:

- **Keep your character busy** with their story goal and their path to satisfaction. It's never boring to see your protagonist do things they shouldn't.
- **Maintain a "judgmental love" of your character with each scene and sequence.** If you're a parent, then you know what I mean. Or if you have a good friend who is always doing things you disagree with, then that's the same attitude you should have with your character. Or maybe your boyfriend/girlfriend/ wife/husband appears deluded about their goals and you always have to adjust to their behavior. Same thing. But this time you are playing master to the story that will "fix" them — either in a good way or leave them with a deep understanding of this flaw.
- **Cause and Effect:** One action or scene must ignite, excite, and affect the next. One ball hitting another ball, hitting another, and another . . . and so on. Energy.
- **You must never give up disagreeing with your character.**
- **Don't put in scenes or beats that are not furthering the story.** Aristotle said it best: "Write what the story demands." A simple idea, but certainly not an easy thing to do. It requires real discipline on your part. I've had a lot of confusion from people on this point. It sounds easy, but it requires your imagination. It means that you must look at your script and ask, "Is this the story?" and if it's not — good-bye! Out it goes! Everything belongs in your script because your screenplay is:

- Thoughtful
- Deliberate
- Purposeful

In other words:

- Everything in your story has been conceived and put there to contribute to the overall value of the experience of the main character.
- Everything in your story was put there by you for a story reason.
- Nothing in your story does not contribute to the journey and conflict of your character.

You are *never not* telling your story.

I hope that's clear even if it is a double-negative.

If your character goes to get lunch for his coworkers, it's for a very good reason (*Three Days of the Condor*).

If your character drops a file folder behind a cabinet . . . (*Being John Malkovich*)

If your character's father has just been shot and he goes to check on his safety at the hospital . . . (*The Godfather*)

All of these examples are carefully thought-out story elements that are placed there in order to fulfill the integrity of the story. The integrity of your story is the integrated and organic cause-and-effect that keeps the story moving forward in time — even if it's all flash-backs. In this way you capture the energy of the character's ordeal and thereby the audience's attention.

This "always telling the story" means that every single morsel of your story has been put there for a reason.

There's no way to hide weak storytelling. You might be able to hide it from an audience, but they will sense that something is wrong.

I guarantee that you cannot hide it from actors. Most actors, if they are looking for a worthwhile acting experience, will simply ask, "How did my character get from there to here?" It's a natural question and if you can't answer it intelligently, then you need to fix that weakness in your story.

My students usually give themselves away when I catch their story napping. Frequently their answer starts with a tepid, "Well, I just . . . " and they follow this with something that has little or nothing to do with the story. It's that "just" that's the dead giveaway. It means they haven't devoted the proper amount of thought and imagination to the action or the cause and effect.

Sometimes they have come up with a nice piece of action or line of dialogue and "just" wanted to throw it in. Or they thought that they might "just" have a mother character in the story. And then I'll ask "Why?" and they will say, "Well, everybody has a mother, don't they?" To which I will counter-query, "Yeah? And what does it have to do with your story?" And then this student will shrug and immediately understand that either they need to connect it to the story or just throw out the material, keeping only what is absolutely necessary.

Stress, Story Torque, and *Zápletka*: Putting the Squeeze On!

Your plot takes your main character through an unfamiliar world. This doesn't mean you need to actually put them in a different geographical location.

Michael Corleone barely leaves home until he's shipped off to Sicily.

In *The Great Beauty* our character travels nowhere farther than the places he's always known in his beloved city of Rome.

In *Three Days of the Condor* Joe Turner is stuck in a city he's called home for many years, yet now everything is different.

Maria travels to Bogota, New Jersey, and New York City, which are places that become progressively less familiar.

In *Der Untergang (Downfall)* Hitler is trapped underground in his bunker for the entire story time. This supposed refuge becomes his tomb.

Additionally, during the protagonist's journey and throughout your whole story, this character is meeting new characters, making new relationships, and if you're doing your job, getting into and out of difficulty. The "out of" part never lasts very long.

All of these elements result in pressure bearing down on these characters and in most cases this is because you've thrown some dramatic and unfamiliar change in their way. What are you going to do to challenge your main character?

In most cases we would call everything that happens the *plot*. I differentiate between this word and the human value they experience as the *story*.

Plot is a handy word. It happens when you connect things, like when you were a kid connecting the dots to reveal a whole drawing. Or when you plan a trip, you plot your course. Or when you scheme against somebody, you plot against him/her. All good. All meaning there is a succession of elements that when connected come to some end result or become a complete form.

The Czechs have another word for it and its meaning is, for me, much stronger than plot. The word is *zápletka*.

For the Czechs it means something else as well. The "tightening" or the "squeezing." It means the gradual buildup of pressure — the *torque* that bears down on a character until the energy buildup is unbearable and BOOM — the climax!

Rather than the old phrase, "The plot thickens," let's say "the plot *tightens*."

Here is the source of the same story energy that we talked about before. Like one of those rubber-band wind-up airplanes. You wind up that rubber band until it ends up in knots. Then you let it go and *whoosh!* — that little plane flies! The tighter you wind it up, the more contorted it becomes, the farther your plane will fly.

Zápletka = story energy.

In physics and engineering they use the word *torque*. It's your job to antagonize your protagonist. It's a way of building *story torque*.

So it is with a good story. You will want to gradually tighten your energy machine until you've created enough energy torque for it to explode. This is why movies take a couple of hours. We need time to develop the story, get all those conflicts going, build up that story torque until you're ready to let go — and *wham!* — all that energy takes off!

One of the pitfalls of storytelling is to make things too easy for your characters. They end up with a small torque energy reserve. There's nothing to use for the climax. I'm sure you've seen these "mild" movies. They're out there. They don't do very well at the box office.

But here's the challenge: treating your character with the same compassion as you would your own child, now's the time to teach your character something. You will do this by thrusting him/her into one difficulty after another. Just when your character gets too comfortable, you throw him/her another jab, then a good gut punch.

Teach them to take care of themselves. What will they do to fight back? How will they cope?

Don't furnish any easy answers. Lay it out like an obstacle course. Make them earn contentment and comfort or else show them in no uncertain terms that their actions come with a price.

This takes a certain kind of spirit when you're writing: you will need to feel the stress of your character, but at the same time you need to be detached because you're deliberately making life difficult for him/her.

But never let up on the pressure. Be brave. Mess up your hero!

Never let your guy/gal get too comfortable. Tempt him/her with new tasks, lure him/her into your traps, and make him/her do stupid crazy things. But in the end, build up the energy you'll need to take this thing over the cliff or down the ski jump of your story.

Eight Good Scenes

> "Give me eight good scenes, and I can make
> a movie . . . " —Howard Hawks

The director of *Bringing up Baby, His Girl Friday, The Big Sleep,* and numerous other classics may have been given to exaggeration. But if anyone was capable of making a movie from a handful of good scenes, it was certainly Hawks. He also had a deep respect for great acting. Remember that combination. He's indisputably correct about one point: any script really must have a handful of memorable scenes. If all you can write is scenes, ultimately they need to be connected together to comprise your story.

Personally, I would like to increase "eight good scenes" to "twelve good scenes." And let's not get hung up on numbers either. There are movies with only one great scene and movies with twenty great scenes. But one thing is true: they have yet to make a great movie with only bad scenes.

Big Tip

Write great scenes that connect in a believable, dramatically engaging manner and you cannot go wrong.

Scenes: The Bricks on the Framework

Good scenes are actually fun to write. They defeat that impatience you get while working on the big picture. Here's where you get to work on the dynamic "small pictures" of your film. You can track moment-to-moment behavior and action and make your characters *do stuff and say stuff.* Scenes are the working activity to get something done during a potentially difficult day at the keyboard. But you will need to connect these little jewels to form a necklace that looks like one thing, not seventy-five pieces of jewelry.

But what's that mean, a "good scene"?

The first thing we'll need to look at is scene structure itself.

Here's something easy to remember:

A *scene* is the action of opposing desires.

Yes, good ol' dramatic conflict. Based upon the reality of your main character's "character," and his/her story personality, what will be his/her response to what has just happened?

Every scene must represent a demand that your character make a choice. However, it must be done within the limits of the world of your character, the character goal (and change) of the story, and the behavior that gives your story plausibility.

A good example is Woody Allen. Allen has for decades (since *Annie Hall*) dedicated himself to the examination of human intimacy, love, marriage, relationships, infidelity, and family. Allen has a knack for pushing his characters into dangerous and uncomfortable emotional territory. The product of his examination becomes comic because his characters speak so bluntly. In a Woody Allen movie it's not unusual for characters to say exactly what's on their minds, sometimes in the most tactless terms.

In one scene in *Crimes and Misdemeanors*, Allen's character has just been told by his divorced and lonely sister about her last date from a personals ad. (On DVD, see: Scene Selection #6 or go to 27:29.)

The sister character is shaking and tearful as she relates the story. It's almost too much for her to tell. She can't stop crying. The story is shown through a short flashback with the sister's voiceover detailing how she met this guy, what a gentleman he was, how they go dancing and have a wonderful hot date. And then coming up to her apartment where she describes how he tied her up and then: "He got on top of me and went to the bathroom on me."

Coming out of the flashback we see Allen's response of absolute shock and repulsion, which is funny by itself. But then the first words out of his mouth are "That is so disgusting! Oh my God! That's the worst thing I've ever heard in my life! You idiot. This guy could have cut your throat." To which his sister replies, "I would have preferred it."

The comedy is increased a notch by this blunt and shocking dialogue, which is just as blunt and shocking as his sister's experience. This is supported by the underlying actions of the characters. This is because we would expect some sympathy from Allen as a brother. These blunt, undisguised emotions bring out the comedy of the moment, but solely because Allen is taking this scene to its outside limit.

By the end of the scene Allen expresses his further shock by saying, "I wish I could have some sympathy for this." But his sister can only reply, "I'm so lonely. You don't know what it's like to be by yourself all the time."

The values in this scene are made more dramatic (and comic) by simply making them direct and very raw. When creating scenes, be very clear about what your characters want and how this fits into your overall story.

Scenes have the same structure as whole stories. Here is a schematic of a typical scene. This schematic uses an example also from *Crimes and Misdemeanors*. It's the scene directly following the one above where Jonah (Martin Landau, the protagonist) a doctor, approaches his brother Jack (Jerry Orbach), a guy who has been on the other side of the tracks in life. Jonah has summoned Jack for help in dealing with his mistress (Anjelica Huston) who is threatening to expose not only his infidelity, but also his possible financial misdeeds.

The greatest drama in this scene is the deep difference in the two brothers. Jonah is a respected ophthalmologist. Jack is from an entirely other world. He refers to his years "with the restaurant, the garment industry and Atlantic City" three places where he got to know some "pretty tough characters."

1. The main character is in this moment for a very clear reason. He has summoned his brother to help him. He's got a big problem in his life. He can't take care of it himself. He needs some "special" help.

2. There is an inciting incident within the first part of the scene. "I heard you wanted to see me about something important. Guess you're in trouble. That's the only time you ever need me." This not only kicks off the scene, but also establishes the conflicts of the brothers. There is a direct candor to all of the dialogue. Our main character has a clear problem; however, the new character will introduce his needs and his problems, confronting our character and causing yet more pressure upon him. When writing a basic two-character scene such as this, you must know this about the scene before you finish it.

3. The scene contains a *call to action*. "My mistress is threatening to expose me. I need your help to take care of it."

4. Within the "second act" of the scene, the underlying conflict — the difference between these two brothers — and the obvious conflict "What am I going to do about this woman?" start to interplay. Then: Jack is insulted that Jonah, the doctor, only calls him when he "needs some dirty work done." This conflict plays out as Jack expresses his anger about being treated so disrespectfully by his brother. Meanwhile,

Dr. Jonah denies almost everything, especially the fact that what he needs is some kind of "final" solution to his problems. This feeds into

5. . . . the climax of the scene. A *flash point* moment, when Jack says, "She can be taken care of. She can be gotten rid of." To which Jonah answers, "This is a human being we're talking about?" The following final beats resolve around the inevitability of Jonah's choice: he doesn't have any. Jonah got what he wanted from Jack, but it goes against everything he believes. What a wonderful, conflicted moment to end on. Now what will he do?

The scene does not resolve on an answer to Jonah's troubles. However, it furthers the story, beat by beat, to reveal the depths that Jonah has fallen to find himself in such a desperate situation. Most importantly, the scene is an outward manifestation and dramatization of Jonah's inner conflict. Remember "praxis"? "The inner psyche of the character pushing outward?" Well here it is, done beautifully (and entertainingly) in my opinion.

Finally, there must be change as there is at the end of any story.

In the end of the above scene, Jonah sees that he has the option to do something terrible. While it puts him into deeper conflict, it also moves us deeper into the action of his story. What's he going to do now? This is what every scene you write must end with.

Each scene must dig a deeper hole for your character, so by the end of Act II, it feels like a grave. Comedies such as *The Hangover* and *Get Him to the Greek* are no exceptions.

Every beat for the Buddies or Aaron Green is fraught with disaster. Whether it's trying to get their kidnapped friend from the crazy Chinese gangster or the moment when Aaron must stick a balloon of heroin into his rectum, these are the extremes that make for memorable, exciting, and entertaining movies.

Cause and Effect: Don't Waste My Screen Time, Pal!

In *The Godfather* Michael Corleone's path to satisfaction is to prove himself worthy to the most important people in his life: his father and his brother Sonny (James Caan).

The story begins with his choice to remain outside his family's "business." In fact, on the day of his sister's wedding, he is waiting to talk to his father and tell him this. He also plans to marry Kay, his non-Italian girlfriend who presents all of the "American" attributes that this son of an immigrant mafioso could bring to put distance between him and his ethnic legacy.

However, he is presented with a series of choices, through natural-seeming scenes and behavior that ultimately push him to choose an utterly different direction. In fact, none of the scenes appear to be unreasonable demands on Michael's choices.

THE GODFATHER

ACT I

1. Michael, a US marine, is asked to be present at his sister's wedding. Sure, what brother would not be?
2. In an extended setup of several sequences — almost a prologue, because it excludes Michael almost completely — we learn how Don Corleone's business works. These choices by the Don cause the first great call to action for our main character, Michael.
3. Don Corleone is shot.
4. Michael rushes to his aid, using his wits (learned as a US Marine) to protect Don Vito from another attempt on his life.
5. Michael now becomes involved in the strategy of what will become a war between the major Mafia factions.
6. Michael agrees to be the assassin to take revenge on those who tried to kill his father.

So in only six major beats, this story is really in the groove!

ACT II

7. Michael is sent away to hide in Sicily, where he experiences a horrible loss when his beautiful young Sicilian wife is assassinated — and it was supposed to be him! Back in the US, his brother Sonny is killed by rival factions.

8. Michael returns to the US, embittered and fully ready to take the reins of his family business. His heart for revenge is fully fledged. He has lost a brother and a lover. He has also lost any will to resist becoming what he did not want to become.

In just this short sequence of events, it's easy to see clearly why these choices are made. The choices made by the Don are made in the interests of "business" while the choices made by Michael are motivated by his feelings for his family. And let's put these two contrasting worlds together and we get the Mafia: a criminal enterprise created under the aegis of "family" yet falsely extolling the integrity of "family."

All of this is built in a sequence of scenes (story beats) that place the main character within a progression of events that meticulously support the ordeal of the film: to either succeed or fail at becoming the Godfather of the Corleone crime family.

I call these choices *gotta*. Your character has *gotta* do it. Any other choice would a) end their ordeal and b) end your dramatic story.

Each scene in *The Godfather* is conscientiously designed to push Michael further and further away from his ideal and closer and closer to the goal he has always resisted. Yet, ironically, it is what his father has always wanted for him (. . . or maybe not).

In one of the most touching scenes near the end of the movie, Michael and his father sit in the garden. A regular, serious father-and-son chat. Again, "family." First, the Don advises his son about a strategy to counter any attempt to dislodge his power by their rivals. Then a few lines about Michael's family and the Don's grandchild (his namesake) Anthony. "Three years old," Michael tells him, "And he already reads the funny papers." The Don returns to advising his son, and of course like any parent, he overdoes it a little bit, causing Michael to comfort him with:

MICHAEL*
What's the matter? What's bothering you?
(the Don doesn't answer)
I'll handle it. I told you I can handle it, I'll handle it.

VITO CORLEONE
I knew that Santino was going to have to go through all this. And Fredo . . . well . . . Fredo was . . . well. But I never . . . I never wanted this for you. I work my whole life, I don't apologize, to take care of my family. And I refused to be a fool dancing on a string, held by all those bigshots. I don't apologize. That's my life. But I thought that . . . that when it was your time that . . . that you would be the one to hold the strings. Senator Corleone. Governor Corleone, or something . . .

MICHAEL
Another pezzonovante . . .

———

*From *The Godfather* screenplay by Francis Ford Coppola and Mario Puzo

The leaps that this scene takes in its three major subjects give it the emotional weight of a great pronouncement for the entire film. Who knew that the Don wanted something else for his son? Where were these words when Michael was ascending to become the rightful heir to his father's empire? The fact is that this is a heartbreaking demonstration and active portrayal of "missed opportunity" for all immigrant Americans. This is Mario Puzo's and Francis Ford Coppola's ironic display that shows that people born with few choices only make the necessary choices that are available for their survival.

This is deeply true for the character of Michael: while it may have appeared that he didn't need to go to his father's aid at the beginning of his journey, it was dramatically and spiritually necessary for the character to do so. So what choice did Michael have? None. Yet, in each beat and every scene of the movie, he must choose one way or the other, and he is compelled by the "gotta" of this masterfully crafted story. As we know, in the Mafia, there is only one choice . . . the Family.

In *Maria Full of Grace*, each and every scene works to underscore Maria's lack of choices. Her personality, which is defiant, independent, diffident, in short, that of a seventeen-year-old, works in partnership with the strong story events.

Placing this character, true to her world, in a poor Colombian town, where the only place to work is the flower factory, screenwriter Josh Marston pushes her toward the inevitable: she must accept the option of becoming a drug mule.

From the very opening of the film, until the last scene, all of the factors that contribute to this story such as Maria's inability to deal with authority and her impulse to act independently conspire to continue the cause-and-effect that bring her to the end, when she realizes that the most important thing is her baby. In fact, Maria is taught to understand a basic part of human existence: to understand what is important in life.

Here's a short scan of *Maria Full of Grace*:

1. Maria works at the flower factory that she hates, especially her mean boss. She's pregnant.
2. She lives with her mother, her sister, her sister's infant son, and her grandmother in a tiny house.
3. She has a not-so-passionate relationship with her boyfriend, Juan.
4. She quits her job.
5. At a village fiesta dance she meets Franklin, a cousin of one of the men who works at her factory
6. She tells her boyfriend, Juan, she's pregnant. Juan is willing to step up, but because they both admit they don't love each other, it's not good enough for Maria.

NOW WHAT?

7. She is about to go to Bogota (the big city) to look for work when Franklin happens by and takes her on his motorcycle, takes her for snacks and drinks and flirts with her in a very gentlemanly way, then tells her that he could find her a job: as a drug mule, smuggling drugs into the US. Then, like a good recruiter, he lays the bait saying, "But this is probably not for you." And that's it.
8. Maria is on the back of his motorbike and they go to meet the drug dealer, a nice old man, who interviews Maria.
9. From here, the movie takes its journey to New York and gives a Maria a really, really tough trip.

If you track this story backward from its ending right back to its first moments, every single cause-and-effect has been built in with real purpose and deliberation. It's one of the most solid and sober screen stories I've ever seen.

When You Pack, Take Only What You're Going to Wear

While we're looking at the traditional restrictions of film, we can compare it to painting: it must fit in the frame. We can also use an analogy to furnishing an apartment. You only have so much room, but you also must have certain amenities if your home is to be comfortable: a living room needs a sofa. A dining area needs a table and chairs.

Screenplays can be looked at in the same way. But let's look at your screen story like a suitcase that you're packing for a trip. First of all, you know your trip is only going to last a certain amount of time. In this case the "trip" is anywhere from 80-140 minutes.

There are all sorts of considerations given to a finished movie's length. Chief among them is cost. The longer the script, the more shooting days, the more locations, the more postproduction and so on.

So even when you don't consider the budget, you must consider size. Let's remember that no matter how long your movie is, it's going to share important qualities with all other movies: main character, problem, journey, climax, and resolution. It will also have a beginning, middle, and end. Those will vary in length and details depending on the story.

But all good films share an important quality: using only what is necessary to tell the story.

I often annoy my students (as you might expect) when they are seeking to quantify their work. Sometimes they are trying to establish some system of metrics and size in determining "how long" or "how much" or "how far."

Aristotle (remember): "Write only what the story demands."

Of course these students are looking for easy answers. If the answers were easy you wouldn't be reading this and I would not have been teaching since 1999.

Writing what the story demands is a pretty simple concept. It's also a demanding principle. This means that just because you feel good about showing your character buying a pack of cigarettes, you must ask yourself: "Is this part of the story?" or "Why is this scene here?"

With this in mind it's important that we understand that you write only what belongs in the story.

Just as you wouldn't take a raincoat on your trip to the desert, you would certainly carefully and thoughtfully make choices and decisions about what you would pack. It has to do with what you will need to wear and use. It also has to do with the size of your suitcase. Everything's got to fit.

Everything you put in your story is not necessarily because you "wanted" it there. This comes as a stern warning: the minute it starts to "feel good" — STOP. Take a deep breath and ask yourself: "What does this mean for the character? Not me." What does it mean for the most important person in your screen story, the protagonist?

This will help define the necessary choices you will need to make, in order to create what I believe is a script that works.

In *Maria Full of Grace*, a film with a seemingly easy, spontaneous, documentary feel, every single element has been carefully placed so that our main character is fully impacted by her experience.

That's right: your story is about the impact of the action on your character. Not you. And (more blasphemy) not the audience.

More weak story decisions have been made in service to pleasing the audience than we can count. This does not mean you ignore your audience. It simply means you drive the story through your main character's experience. This will increase the audience's involvement. It will also ensure that they will feel just like your main character.

At the end of *The Godfather* I believe we feel horrified at what Michael has become.

At the end of *Chinatown* we should feel absolutely hopeless; that the world can't be changed no matter what we do.

At the end of *The Hangover* we probably feel relieved and a bit chastened. While it's fun to have fun, there's such a thing as "too much fun" — because what's important is friendship and family.

All of these stories achieve their impact because of the necessary elements they include as well as the unnecessary ones they exclude.

For instance, in *The Godfather* there is never any meandering. Each scene is a response to the previous one. Usually it's because Michael has chosen to do something. Why? Because a police chief punched him in the face. So what's he going to do about it? He's going to convince his older brother, Sonny, and the chief consigliore, Tom, that he is the one who should perform the assassination.

In the next scene, he is coached by one of his father's longtime mob partners. This is where he learns of the plan for the gun hidden in the washroom, behind one of those old toilets. How is this known? Another of his father's partners knows the old restaurant where they will meet.

The next scene is the men waiting to get word from their "inside" man about the location and time. Anything can go wrong.

The next scene is Michael in the car with the police chief and the mobster who engineered the attempt on his father's life.

The next scene is the tense dinner. The three men sit and all the while we are experiencing Michael's fear and tension.

Looking at this little beat sheet you can see how carefully planned this was. Of course any assassination is well planned. But from the point of view of the main character, this adds to the tension and excitement of the entire sequence, which climaxes in one of the greatest murder scenes in any mob movie.

But notice how lean the sequence is. There isn't a moment that isn't relevant to the story. There's nothing extra, nothing atmospheric.

Please don't think this is some clinical approach. There is a way to include the simple atmosphere of the world of your story.

Maria Full of Grace has a really terrific "necessity" scene dressed up as a simple party scene.

It follows fast on the heels of Maria's fight with her mother and sister over quitting her job. What's she going to do now? "In this town, there are only flowers," her mother tells her.

That night at a town dance, with a terrific local band, she and her boyfriend and their young friends toast her defiant (and pretty foolish) act. Maria, feeling good, helps her best friend, Blanca, meet the guy who's had his eye on her at the flower factory.

This guy introduces them to his cousin, Franklin.

So far, this all seems kind of slapped together. Just a party scene. Pretty irrelevant. Like a screenwriter putting in an unnecessary musical sequence just to fill time and maybe get a little more "atmosphere" out of the setting of the story.

But writer/director Josh Marston is actually packing in a ton of important stuff in this scene. It's almost like a "story party" in its own way.

As Maria attempts to dance with her drunken boyfriend, Juan, he's too drunk and spins her around too fast. She's pissed off and walks away from him.

At that moment, Franklin asks her to dance. Unnecessary? Not at all. This is his job, to find vulnerable, susceptible young women to become drug mules!

The next day, on his cool motorcycle, Franklin spots Maria taking a bus to the city. He offers her a ride. They stop for fruit drinks on the highway and it is here, on a quiet mountain roadside, that he makes his proposition: become a drug mule. Make big money. You won't get caught. Only stupid people get caught and you're too smart and too pretty to get caught.

And within a few moments, Maria has said, "How much?" and the next cut she's on Franklin's motorbike heading to see the head drug guy in Bogota, the capital city.

It's those tiny details that lead Maria and push the story in this all-important direction. Without these small events we would not get to our biggest event, Maria agreeing to be a drug mule.

All of it occurs naturally and seems organic to the story. But in fact it is a painstaking arrangement of each stitch in the cloth of this story.

All of this is based upon the values that you intend to communicate through your story. Your thoughtfulness must now carry through to every detail of the sequence of events — the cause-and-effect that propels us to the compelling revelation of your story.

Irony: It's Not Over 'til It's Not Over

We've established that you, the writer, will make everything in your story meaningful.

But don't confuse this with the idea that you're going to write so that the meaning is absolutely obvious. Nor are you deliberately obscuring the meaning. What you're doing is showing how difficult it is for your characters to understand their own actions.

While movies portray life, they are not actually life. They are an organized dramatization designed to make some kind of point about life and the continuous struggle to be better human beings (even when the heroes are apes!). Characters in your story never really understand what they are doing until after they have done it. Just as an audience cannot really know what your story is about until it comes to an end — or not.

If they're robbing a bank with their loose-cannon partner (*The Town)*, then the lead character doesn't understand his choices until after it's too late. By the same token, when he promises his girlfriend that this is it, he doesn't really understand that what will actually happen will be the utter opposite of that promise. The bank job will be a disaster. He will not gain any freedom at all after committing this crime.

Every need you establish for your character will be met with an obstacle. In many cases, it's an obstacle that we (in everyday life) would be aware of well before attempting to confront it.

While this is how your middle goes, it can also be the way your ending ends. A resonant kind of ringing in the ears (or the mind) after your story ends.

Remember, your protagonist's awareness is somewhat limited. Imagine that he/she has tunnel vision. (Okay, some of you may simply need to imagine them as one of your parents!) Your protagonist can only see his/her goal. Now you, the writer, come in and steer him/her in all the wrong directions. You make your character want things he/she can't really have — at least not very easily.

In the end, if you're doing your job, their gain will also be their loss.

Of course we see that in *Chinatown* and *The Godfather (I & II)*.

Jake Gittes thinks he can take on the most powerful people in Los Angeles and at the same time rectify the blunders of his past. But in the end — HA! — it's quite the opposite. He undoes everything and causes tragedy. Even he can't understand it at the end, but we do. We're shaking our heads, wagging our fingers at him: "You shouldn't have been so overconfident." Then again, he really wanted to do the right thing. But in the end the right thing turned out to be absolutely wrong.

One dictionary definition of *irony* is "a literary technique, originally used in Greek tragedy, by which the full significance of a character's words or actions are clear to the audience or reader although unknown to the character."

Sound familiar?

The word, having nothing to do with the metal, is taken from the Greek *eirēneía*, meaning "dissimulation" or, "fake ignorance." It's the way we don't see what's right in front of our eyes. It's the way your character runs headlong into conflict.

Oedipus? Oh, the irony!

Irony is only possible in art and literature. That's because in our physical world, the simultaneous occurrence of opposites in the same space is impossible.

However, irony demands that this contrast of two opposites be present at a particular moment, or thematically perceived in a story.

It produces a wincing, head-shaking, life-questioning kind of existential feeling. In fact, existentialism itself as a philosophy claims, "Hey man, there's no real purpose to this thing called 'life,' so why make such a big deal?"

But your story does make a big deal. Your story is supposed to be this warning to your character (and your audience).

In *The Godfather(s)* Michael Corleone believes he's striving for justice (avenging his father's name) and for power (strengthening his empire against his enemies). But it's not what we would recognize as either. He's a deceitful murderer who destroys his marriage, kills his own brother, and consolidates his business enterprises through violence and avarice. By the end of *The Godfather, Part II* Michael is at the absolute pinnacle of his power and is now completely and utterly alone. His quest to consolidate his family has resulted in a victory of his criminal enterprise and a complete defeat of his soul.

This dramatic irony is a quality shared by what I consider to be the best movies.

When my son was about nine years old we went to see Disney's animated *The Road to El Dorado*. This animated adventure took two hapless con artists, fleeing their last failed scam, to deepest Mexico where they hid out in what appeared to be a magical kingdom of the Aztecs, El Dorado, literally, the "City of Gold." This was the mythical spot that all men dreamed of. A place where gold ran like water.

So there they were. Instead of trying to integrate themselves into this society, their first instinct (their "pathology"; their "character deficit") drove them to make it a scam. They simply didn't know how to be good guys.

As the story progresses, their scam works. The people think they are gods and shower them with gold. One of them falls in love with the beautiful princess. Looks like El Dorado will be the place to just stay forever.

Then they learn that Hernando Cortes, the merciless conqueror from Spain, is headed to El Dorado to plunder it and slaughter everyone.

In the end, the two guys are able to shut the magic stone wall, saving El Dorado but sealing it off forever from the world — and from their gold. They get away with nothing — no gold, no princess — except the good deed that they have saved El Dorado.

At the end of the movie, as the lights in the theater came up, my nine-year-old called out: "That was really ironic!" After getting over how stunned I was, I asked him, "Why?"

And he very correctly told me: "Because all they wanted was the gold, but in the end they ended up doing a much better thing, but they didn't get the gold."

And I said, "But they did the right thing." To which the proper answer is: "But they didn't get the gold."

Also notice that the path to satisfaction was defeated by the change in the characters.

A solid ironic ending like this never really ends. That's why it's called *irony*. Because it seals the story in a kind of never-ending ending. The "but" can be said over and over and you'll never get to any kind of result.

That's the hallmark of a great story.

A lack of irony is actually the hallmark of a lousy story. There are places where non-ironic stories are very, very successful — TV soap operas.

I don't think there is anything wrong with them. They can be very popular. But there is a pronounced lack of irony. And like a lack of humor, it can also mean a lack of complexity.

When a nine-year-old can appreciate irony as part of his entertainment experience, you can bet that a vast majority of the audience appreciates it as well.

Action films actually present some of the best examples.

In *Dawn of the Planet of the Apes* (2014), the ultimate irony is that humans cannot teach beasts to be less bestial! War, violence, and tyranny are part of any society that tries to be organized. Isn't that ironic? The more organized we want to be, the more risk we take in falling into chaos. That's because civilization involves leadership. And leadership is power. And power . . . ? Power is very, very complicated!

Irony is not simply the "but" that summarizes the action and value in a script; it's also a bit of a wink, a nudge, and a wise nod. It's the moment we realize that change comes at a price. Any reward also comes with punishment. Any win means loss.

In *Silver Linings Playbook,* Pat (Bradley Cooper) can't see that the woman who really loves him is not his ex-wife, but Tiffany (Jennifer Lawrence). Yet all he really wants is to get back together with his ex-wife. He even makes a deal with Tiffany to help him, never really understanding until the end that it is Tiffany he loves after all. What a dope! But now, a better guy having gone through this whole ordeal.

In *Get Him to the Greek* Aaron (Jonah Hill) learns that simply being loyal to your idol is not what life is all about. One must have a healthy relationship, pay attention to the needs of your loved ones, and be a principled person. All of these values are learned after an arduous, drug-filled, sometimes dangerous and always hilarious journey. Noah soon sees that this was a bad choice, but it's too late. He must get Aldous to the Greek Theater or his entire plan, his boss's plan, and his job will be a bust.

He does it, but in the end he realizes that it didn't matter about Aldous. What matters is being with his wife. It's ironic that this lesson came so late for him, but if he had not taken his journey, there would have been no impact for him. Understanding his own problems only occurred when he came to understand Aldous' problems. He was blinded by his path to satisfaction: reviving Aldous' career.

The greatest irony can occur in tragedy.

In *Chinatown* Jake Gittes' overconfidence as a detective makes him the perfect victim of his own hubris. Thinking he can take on the most powerful (and evil) forces in Los Angeles, he believes he can not only straighten out the city and bring these villains to justice, but also avoid repeating the misdeeds of his past.

In the end, he not only fails to defeat his antagonists, but also clearly fails to avoid another tragedy: hurting someone close to him . . . just like always.

It's clearly ironic that a guy who was simply trying to do the right thing does precisely the opposite. His recognition in the final moments of the film brings him to a mental and physical standstill.

I can't talk about irony without referring to *Oedipus Rex*. Here is a hero who is determined to defeat his own destiny, but in fact does nothing less than seal it. If that's not irony, I don't know what is. This play by Sophocles is probably the longest running hit in history. It was over 160 years old when Aristotle studied it. That's because its irony is deeply compelling. Audiences eat it up!

From the start of the story the audience is cringing on Oedipus' behalf at his audacity in defying the oracle and seeking to change his destiny. Yet his ironic misadventure is riveting. Will he do it? Of course he won't! But won't it be great drama just watching him try.

Bicycle Thieves is really one of the great tragic ironies. It's all in the title, isn't it? By the end of the film who is the real bicycle thief? Irony can really cut deep. In the final moments of the film, De Sica makes a stunning edit to the face of Antonio's son as his father speeds away on the bicycle he's stolen. After their amazing journey, the little boy has finally come to respect his father. But now he looks across the street and sees the end of his father. A man utterly broken by his own pride and the realities of their world. Good irony should be heartbreaking.

Be aware of the potential for irony when you begin conceiving your story. If you're on the right track, it will occur naturally. Irony is a natural human response to the world. When you're trying to get something into the thick skull of your protagonist, it'll be a wonderful moment when they finally get it, despite their lack of judgment, their selfishness and self-delusion. "I've been a fool!" they will cry, and even if they don't pluck out their own eyes, the feeling will reverberate long after the story ends.

What's the Worst That Can Happen? — That's What Happens!

In a good card game, when you sit down at the table, you want the assurance that you have the opportunity to win a lot of money. Let's not forget, that means you stand to lose a lot of money as well.

Stakes. That's what makes things important. They also fuel your *zápletka* and the overall pressure you put on your protagonist.

Movies are no exception. Stakes are the determining factor in how we respond to your character's journey. I wouldn't encourage anyone without experience to sit down at a high-stakes game of poker. However, if the stakes in your movie are too low, your story energy will also be low. The risks your character is taking will have no significance and in the end the response to the story will be tepid both from the audience and from your character.

As in *Crimes and Misdemeanors,* the idea is that if you put extremely opposed elements together, you can generate the proper energy almost by default. It is the energy of all of these extremes that collide to maintain our interest as well as push the story forward: The Woody Allen character wants to end his marriage and take up with Mia Farrow's character. In the twin story, a rich and respected eye doctor (Martin Landau) has entangled himself in an illicit, passionate affair that risks his marriage and his professional reputation. He must do something for the sake of his very existence.

Let's look at *The Hangover.*

Three friends wake up after a bachelor party night in Las Vegas to find they remember nothing of the night before. Their groom-to-be buddy is gone. A tiger is in their bathroom. An abandoned infant is in their room. When they ask for their car from the parking valet, he brings a Las Vegas Police cruiser. When they get their hands on the Mercedes they had driven to Vegas, a naked Chinese man pops out of the trunk and runs off.

And that's just Act I!

What's great about *The Hangover* is that the writers waste no energy in pumping up the extremes of the movie's stakes. If anything, all of the evidence the friends find in Act I is ultimately resolved, but not until after a ridiculously wild, dangerous, and funny journey.

The Hangover is like a good mystery. This search ordeal results in not only putting everything right, but also reinforces their friendship and helps them all go on to become better people and real friends, not just "crazy bachelor party" friends. And it's a very funny movie (or at least I think so and so did audiences who made it the tenth highest grossing film of 2009).

Many of my students fall into a trap in their scripts. It's a set of actions and conflicts that are altogether mild and everyday. Even the elements of description are as un-compelling as "sort of good looking" or "he's a typical guy, nothing special, nothing terrible."

That is a probably non-special, typical un-terrible place to start. In other words, it's dull. It lacks story energy. When you look at the opening of *The Hangover* you are moved to say "These guys are in a really, really terrible situation," not "These guys are in a kind of typical normal situation and all they have to do is call room service and it will be straightened out."

BIG YAWN.

Your story must necessarily be composed of a succession of extremes that pit your main character against the obstacles and setbacks that will push the ordeal and the journey to some significant realization and/or change.

In *Maria Full of Grace* Maria doesn't simply hate her job, she quits! She doesn't simply find herself between jobs — she's screwed! What's she going to do next? She is the sole breadwinner in her family and now Maria's actions are threatening their well-being.

And let's not forget . . . she's pregnant!

High stakes.

Michael Corleone is not going to sit down and negotiate with his mob enemies, including a police chief, he's going to kill them.

In *Apollo 13* our guys are not just stuck. If they don't solve their problems, they will die.

In *Flight*, ace pilot Whip Whitaker (Denzel Washington) isn't just a guy with a drinking and drug problem; he's completely messed up on coke and weed when he gets behind the wheel of a fully loaded passenger jet and then he crashes his plane! Now he must go through a complete investigation of his actions — which will push him to do an inventory of himself and come to some startling and life-changing conclusions (which he certainly does!).

These extremes must necessarily be installed in the entire journey of your story. Without them, your story energy will not be sustainable, your characters will cease to struggle, and your story will fall apart.

I know this happens a lot in most of the movies we see.

Some call it "story fatigue." Others call it "second act-itis." I call it lazy (or bad) storytelling.

Part of solving this problem is a creative process that leads you to making more courageous decisions with your story development. It's not only time to scale the wall, it's time to make the wall higher.

I say this because in one of the world's most beloved space adventures, *Star Wars*, our hero Luke Skywalker must face the worst villain in the universe, Darth Vader. Why? Because Luke is a direct threat to Darth and his plan to conquer and destroy the Federation.

But the battle is not simply about good v. evil. Ironically, Darth Vadar turn out to be Luke's father.

Father was willing to murder his son to conquer the universe. The son must kill the father in order to save the Federation (and the galaxy) but also take his place as a full-fledged Jedi Fighter, i.e., earn his full manhood.

Now that's what I'm talkin' about! Writer-director George Lucas was not shy about pushing this to the extremes he needed to create energy, drama, and excitement. I believe it was this final twist at the end that makes the audience gasp. "His father? Oh no!"

Same with *Chinatown*. While we believe that Noah Cross's plot is evil — to buy land in the name of dead people and make millions when the land is merged with the City of Los Angeles — the act of raping his own daughter and finally wanting to have possession of the offspring from this repellent act takes evil to a whole new level.

Robert McKee calls this, most appropriately, the "negation of the negation."

The idea is that just when you thought things were going badly — hang on — they're going to get worse!

This is especially true, and necessary, in horror movies. Just when we thought it was safe, *wham*, here comes another, bigger monster!

Let's remember the very last moments of *Carrie* (the classic 1976 original directed by Brian De Palma). After Carrie has unleashed her murderous adolescent anger in a bloody rampage, she's finally stopped and killed. As the camera slowly moves in on her gravestone, *boom*!, her bloody hand reaches up out of the dirt with the promise of more revenge . . . or at least a sequel.

Back to Oedipus: "Not only will you kill your father, you're going to have sex with your mother." If this was good enough for Greece in 389 BC, you can bet it is good enough for us today.

Your first task in coming up with your idea is putting your character in a "life and death" situation.

Even in Kubrick's *Barry Lyndon* our main character's raw opportunism pushes the stakes higher and higher until he finds himself in a duel with his own stepson. His injury in the duel leads to the amputation of his leg and a life of continued misery.

Kubrick was the expert at this in all of his films. I call this *romancing the negative*. His films deprived us of that all-important emotional purging, the catharsis, that audiences really love. Playwright Bertolt Brecht was also a master of this. Neither of these artists wanted to free the audience from the misery of their own lives, but rather, drive home the point that the audience is an accomplice in the miseries of our society, leaving them in a state of despair.

Hey, it still sells tickets.

Kubrick is more like Sophocles than Euripides. He doesn't care about happy endings. In fact, his only comedy, *Dr. Strangelove or: How I Learned to Stop Worrying and Love the Bomb* produced the most bizarre and shattering punch line in movie history: "We're going to blow up the planet and in the last few seconds a cowboy air force pilot will ride the A-bomb down to ground zero whoopin' and hollerin' the whole way down."

Funny? Yes. To the 1964 audience and to this day it's a hilarious moment in movies. How better to portray the folly and tragedy of mutually assured destruction.

But Kubrick (and screenwriter Terry Southern and book author Peter George) wanted to show just how close we were to nuclear war and total destruction. This isn't a story about the heroic prevention of nuclear apocalypse. It's the story of how stupid and wasteful nuclear weapons actually are. Rather than showing the characters gallantly arriving at peace, *Dr. Strangelove* uses absolute tragedy and destruction to show us who we really are: stupid, incompetent children who have the power of total self-destruction.

Your Surprise Ending . . . Is Inevitable

Everybody is always talking about that "twist" at the end of a movie. Think about it. Who is that twist really for? If you guessed "the main character," I would agree with you.

So many screenwriters (new ones especially) think you need to come up with some big surprise twist or reversal at the end of the movie for the sake of keeping an audience excited. I might agree, except that let's remember whom we are writing this script for: the main character.

Let's look at a few famous surprising endings.

In *Casablanca* Rick (Humphrey Bogart) is a man who has decided to escape from the world by opening a restaurant in the exotic and far-off city of Casablanca. Why? We soon learn he's mending a broken heart. He was in love . . . once. And it ended badly. He's decided he doesn't want any more unhappy endings in his life. So when the story begins, he's living a noncommittal life as the host and proprietor of Casablanca's coolest joint, Rick's Café Américain.

I believe if you've read this far that you can guess where I'm going with this. If you set up a character who is determined to stay away from commitment and relationships, what are you going to do to create drama and change? What kind of journey and ordeal is this character going to be put through?

That's right. You're going to set him on a journey that pushes him to reverse all of those experiences that caused him to withdraw. By the end of the movie Rick Blaine has not only once again found his one true love, but he will also become a hero who plays a small role in saving the Western world.

But not before he goes through a rigorous ordeal that will gradually and irreversibly bring him to one of the most famous surprise endings in movie history.

Here are the major elements that set up Rick for the marvelous last moments:

- He's a determined loner, always certain to stay away from love and commitment. We see this in the opening minutes when he rejects one of the many women who are after his affections. We also see him sacrifice a friend and customer (Peter Lorre) to the Nazi-complicit gendarmes. He's not going to help anybody (see below) who doesn't deserve it.
- He's given up any political affiliations. We learn in a conversation that he was rumored to have been a gunrunner in Spain for the antifascists. Or had he been part of the French

underground in Paris? But we hear him say in no uncertain terms, "I stick my neck out for nobody." Here is a terrific example of what Shakespeare would say: "Methinks he doth protest too much!" In other words, if you're really comfortable with who you are, why make such a big deal about it? This is the amazing reverse psychology that is at the roots of this wonderful screen story. The story torque is constantly maintained by Rick's unwillingness to move in the direction of his change. It's difficult. It's filled with conflict.

- Then, *boom*!, his lost love, Ilsa, walks into his club. No, she's not there looking for him; she's there because Casablanca is the only place in the world where her husband, Victor Laszlo, will be safe. He's a wanted anti-Nazi underground leader and that's why they're in Casablanca. He's been kicked out of Czechoslovakia and he's on the run. This is the man who stole her away from Rick in Paris. This is the man who Ilsa left Rick for, the rain washing away the ink on her "Dear Rick . . . " note of farewell at the Paris train station (which produced another great line from the movie, "We'll always have Paris").

- By Act I we learn that only Rick has the influence to get Victor and Ilsa out of Casablanca to neutral Lisbon where Victor can continue the good fight. Why this is true is never fully explained, but here is a great example of "Zombie Rules" or "along for the ride." We don't care if it's true. We accept as much as we can in order to be involved in the story. The magic of fiction!

- So the big question is: Will Rick follow his path to satisfaction by winning back Ilsa and sending Victor to the Nazi wolves? Or will he do what his old self would have done — save the world?

- In the end, after we add the torque of the pressure on Rick and we follow him through this arduous ordeal of will-he-or- won't-he, Rick is confronted with the final choice.

- This final moment is not only a sudden reversal for Rick but also for the chief of police, the easily reversible Louis Renault.
- Finally, confronted with everything in the story experience and because there is a promise of change, Rick kills the Nazi commandant and is saved at the last second when Louis says, "Round up the usual suspects." (One of the great "plant-and-payoff" lines in movie history. See: Chapter 7.)

But is it really any big surprise that Rick has come to this decision? We learn, slowly but surely, what kind of man he was and more importantly, what kind of man he wishes to be. So while the ending is a delicious and exciting surprise, it makes perfect sense and appears to be inevitable. Here are a few other endings we could have had:

- Rick joins the Nazis and lives a comfortable life as an informant in Casablanca.
- He keeps Ilsa in Casablanca where they live a bitter married life knowing they turned in Victor Laszlo and thus set the stage for a worldwide Nazi victory.
- Rick doesn't get involved. He doesn't "stick his neck out" and allows the natural forces of his world to make the choices for him. Victor is somehow arrested. Ilsa is taken to a concentration camp. Rick moves to London after the war where he opens another successful restaurant and lives guilt-free knowing he did not interfere with anyone else's fate.

Based on all the story circumstances presented in the movie, any of these could certainly be possible.

But probable?

None of the above is satisfying in any way. None presents any promise of change. None is very dramatic. None of the above would actually begin until the movie we know as *Casablanca* would be over. Finally, those three scenarios would be about a guy who does not change. And yes, Stanley Kubrick may have made any one of them. But let's admit it, as an audience we would be assured of some bitter moments in the experience.

So, your so-called surprise ending is really no surprise at all — except for the characters.

With the groundwork you've completed:

- The value of your story
- The main character's path to satisfaction
- The world of your character's journey
- The life-and-death stakes that create pressure (*zápletka*) on your character
- The consequences for your character if they should fail.
- The reward for your character if they succeed.

You are now ready to move ahead to tell a compelling, exciting, entertaining, and satisfying story.

EXERCISE

Before deciding to start on your idea, make certain you have a life-and-death arc for your story. This is not easy! Most of your ideas will make you feel good because they feel funny. Or you'll have an idea that you feel is sure to move or frighten your audience. But if you don't put your characters into some kind of jeopardy, your story will not have sufficient energy to move anyone.

Once again, think of your characters.

In your character biography list three things that your character is most afraid of. (Sorry, but you can't list "death." That's something you might be afraid of, but let's leave it off the list for now.) However you can list "combat" or "confrontation" or "love."

Chapter 7

....

TOOL BAG: SOME OF THE GADGETS YOU'LL NEED

YOU'RE PROBABLY ASKING: What about all that other stuff like flashbacks and voiceover and backstory and ally characters and all that?

Because these are like little gadgets you pull out when you need them, it all depends on what story you are telling and how you want to tell it. Remember? "There are no rules in screenwriting, but you have to obey every single one."

This is like knowing how to make a certain joint in carpentry or using a particular angle for the roof of the house you are building or understanding the tempo you want a piece of music. Since you have now decided on what your story is about, it is now a question of how you are going to tell it. You're making something very similar to something else; however, it will have a different shape, color, and impact on the user. Here are some of the "gadgets" that will help. As always, you will need to be thoughtful about using them.

"Shut Up When You Talk to Me . . . " Dialogue Is Not Just Talk

So many people will say, "I write great dialogue. I could be a terrific screenwriter." If you've gotten this far in the book, you know what my response will be. Your response should be: "That's nice, but dialogue is not necessarily storytelling and it isn't really a deciding factor in the aptitude of a future screenwriter. It's true, if you write crappy dialogue or don't have any skill at it, I would say your prospects as a screenwriter are nil.

It was Alfred Hitchcock who said that a good story is "life with the dull parts taken out." It's similar with dialogue. Sure, it's conversation — but it's *the* conversation not just *a* conversation.

This exchange of language between two characters must enunciate the conflict between them. But it's not just an argument or a verbalized disagreement. As we learned in the scene from *Crimes and Misdemeanors* characters are not just talking, they are jockeying for power. But the trick is to not make every exchange of dialogue a pitched battle inspired by the values in your story. It's a normal conversation, but each character is thinking about something very important and can't end this exchange until someone has made some progress or until one character admits defeat.

But it's not just talk. Yes, some of the best movies have a ton of dialogue — both *Godfathers, Chinatown, Being John Malkovich, Election, The Bicycle Thief.* Then again when you look at movies like *Eraserhead* and *Jules et Jim* you'll find a devastating muteness. That's because every story makes its own demands on how the story will be told. Whether to make your script dialogue-intensive is dictated by so many different factors. The good news is that dialogue almost takes care of itself. If your script feels like it's going to be a dialogue-friendly story, then the decision is made as you write. But I feel there are some important values to understand before you just start making your characters blab.

Dialogue is a like a drug. It's easy to use to convey information to an audience. But it's not sound storytelling. Dialogue is a delicate little monster. Like a touchy pet, it can bite you if you let it get out of your control. The first step in understanding dialogue is actually avoiding it until it is absolutely necessary.

It's easy to suddenly get your character to explain something, even if it's to another character. Your first question should be: "Can

I show this?" If you can show it, then *show* it, don't *say* it!

The next thing you need to understand is why these two characters are in this scene in your story. This decision has already been
made purposefully and thoughtfully by you because it wouldn't be
there unless it was absolutely necessary to your story. If you've constructed this segment of action according to the right specifications,
then the dialogue is secondary to the scene. The dialogue is something that one character must say to the other.

In *Chinatown* Gittes and Mrs. Mulwray meet for lunch. In the
scene Gittes questions her closely, trying to persuade her that they
are on the same side; that whoever set up Gittes in this false investigation also set up Mrs. Mulwray's husband.

Throughout this very talky scene, Gittes is simply doing his
job. The scene concludes in a dispute. Mrs. Mulwray gets mad and
excuses herself. Gittes' goal in the scene remains unsatisfied, but
then, suddenly, Mrs. Mulwray changes her mind and before she
speeds off in her car, she hires Gittes to work for her.

Throughout the scene we're following and listening to Gittes as
he attempts to steer the woman to his point of view. But in fact, Mrs.
Mulwray is way ahead of him and in the end, while appearing negative she acts to stop his inquiry by doing something surprisingly
positive, yet is it?

Of course, at the end of the scene Gittes is in more of a quandary
than he was at the beginning. In the process, we've learned of Gittes'
theories in the case and then had them blown out of the water by
his subject.

Another great dialogue scene in *Chinatown* is when Gittes arrives
to confer with the new head of the water department. He's given
the runaround by a middle-aged, glowering, and easily annoyed
secretary.

As time passes, with Gittes sitting quietly, smoking a cigarette,
deliberately annoying the secretary, the tension of the silence builds.
Then Gittes gets up to stretch his legs a bit and takes a look at some

photos on the wall. He's only trying to annoy the secretary so she'll get fed up with him.

The men in the photos are key characters in the story, Hollis Mulwray and Noah Cross. As Gittes circles the pictures, he also asks questions — still trying to annoy the secretary. In the process he (and we!) get a full history of the Los Angeles water system and the long friendship and falling out of these two powerful personalities. In the end the secretary has had enough. She gets her boss to see Gittes, just as he had planned.

In this case master screenwriter Robert Towne has turned his subtext and super-text inside out. Gittes hasn't come to find out the history of the department. However, he's staging a kind of sit-in on the secretary to get in to see the new commissioner. He accomplishes both! But the action of the scene is to annoy the secretary. He accomplishes both of these underlying actions and the by-product is a complete history of LA's water from an almost unbiased source. This is brilliant use of dialogue.

It's impossible to think of all the different problems you'll face writing dialogue. But here are a few things you need to keep in mind:

- Don't write obvious exposition. For example, in the above scene, don't have the secretary willingly volunteer the information.
- The characters can talk about one thing (*super-text*: the actual spoken words), but mean something else (*subtext*: the real meaning beneath the spoken words).
- The opposite of the above is "on the nose" dialogue where characters say exactly what they are feeling inside. Don't do it!
- Watch your profanity. Sure, if your characters use foul language as part of their culture, that's okay. But profanity in most dialogue is like a gunshot. Use it sparingly and only when completely necessary. It also affects the ratings of a

movie and therefore its economic exposure. Think about it carefully.

- Unless you're using it for comic effect, don't use cliché dialogue like "You're the son I never had" or "Every dog gets his day" or "That's the way life goes sometimes."
- Don't get stuck on people exchanging chit-chat like "Hi, how are you?" "Fine, how are you?" "Fine. I had a hard day at the office." Of course, David Lynch has terrific fun with this type of superficial language. But he uses it for satiric purposes to show characters in denial about their real feelings.

In a stage play spoken words are very important. That's because plays are written for us to hear how the character is feeling. But in movies, it's more important to understand what a character is *thinking* and how the spoken words will hide it. It's not what they're saying, it's what they're feeling and not saying.

"Many Years Ago . . . " — Flashbacks

This is probably the most used (and overused) gadget in the tool bag. We all understand that your story takes place now. So how do you include and dramatize important past events in a character's journey now?

The *flashback* in storytelling goes back as far as the *Odyssey* (700 BC). This story is told by Odysseus to a listener (presumably Homer, the author) and so is recounted as one long flashback of the actual events of the story. In *The Arabian Nights* (c. 622 AD), the first moments tell of a discovery of a dead woman. We then move back to previous events to learn the answer to the mystery.

It's difficult not to come up instantly with ten movies that use flashbacks. *Casablanca* has one of the most famous — Rick's memories of his love affair in Paris with Ilsa.

It would be hard to imagine the story of *Courage Under Fire* told without the flashbacks. This taut and competent military courtroom

drama is all about finding out what happened during a rescue operation in Iraq during Desert Storm. The flashbacks are exciting as each
witness recounts a slightly different story Who's lying? Who's telling
the truth? Whose memory is reliable?

In fact, throughout the story we ask, "What happens to someone's
memory when he/she is under great stress, like being under fire?"
Finally, a significant part of the story is the struggle of the lead inves-
tigator, Col. Sterling (Denzel Washington) to understand his own
problems of courage and if he has the right to judge other soldiers
who showed courage.

The flashbacks are not the main event. In this story we are always
reminded of the now. But the flashbacks are presented through
the filter of Col. Sterling and how they are making him feel in the
present-day time frame. These flashbacks are not being presented
for simple information but also to compound the *zápletka* of the
story torque. The more Sterling learns, the harder it becomes to
make a decision. Ultimately we are led to ask the question: "What is
the truth . . . really?"

Can you imagine the Kurosawa classic *Rashomon* without flashbacks? It is composed of four long flashback segments all recounting a possible rape in the woods. But who's telling the truth? Much
like *Courage Under Fire*, for those involved, simply giving testimony
amounts to a mangling and misunderstanding of the truth. In the
end the characters come away with a deeper doubt in themselves
and their memories as well as a skeptical vision of "the truth." But
those flashbacks give the movie its plot and help to build up dramatic
pressure and energy.

One could say that *The Hangover* uses Mike Tyson's security video
as a flashback. However, we get to see the guys experience their
memory when they watch it. They're shocked! And it's another dis-
turbing trauma they experience on the way to resolving their main
problem — finding their friend. How clever, right?

So why do screenwriters and filmmakers try to avoid flashbacks?

The biggest reason is that a story well told takes place *now*. Our journey of moving to the satisfying conclusion shouldn't be delayed in time. It can also mean you're asking your audience to keep track of a lot of story. Certainly the above examples make that demand, but that's up to you too.

Think of "story time" in your script as a string. If you pull that string taut and straight there's more tension. There's a direct, unbroken connection between beginning, middle, and end. This is sustained time tension. If we travel along that string in continuous time, it is a very dynamic experience. But what happens if you stop on your string, to present events (and string!) that happened before? You're breaking the string. You have to retie when you come back to the now.

My favorite adaptation, *Dr. Jekyll and Mr. Hyde*, is originally a flashback story. In the Robert Louis Stevenson novella, the story is recounted by Jekyll to a neighbor who in turn recounts the story to us. Luckily, Hollywood screenwriters understood that the real story was the *now story* of Jekyll. The neighbor's experience had no impact on the now of the story and has never been a part of any dramatic adaptation of this great masterpiece of literature.

Crappy flashbacks can be found in some movies, but luckily not many. Screenwriters seem to avoid them and more times than not avoid placing cheap and cheesy gadgets into their movies. Sometimes seeing how others do the right thing is the best way to learn to do the right thing yourself.

My best advice for flashbacks is that whatever is being recalled must have a direct effect on the characters in the present. This can be the revelation of a secret. This can be the exposure of deceit. This can be one character revealing a hard truth to another. And as I've shown, it can be how the listener or "receiver" of the flashback uses this information and what the response in the main character's story is.

In the end I believe you will need to give some serious thought to how you will use a flashback and, most importantly, ask yourself: Is it necessary? The reason you can't just throw in a flashback is:

a) Your story should always take place now. This means events in the now affect your character's journey in the normal linear time of your story.

b) There are so many ways to bring the past into your now story (see following "Backstory" section). Sometimes a single line can accomplish what a two-minute flashback might only deflate.

Backstory: How Does It Get into My (Front) Story?

What is this thing we call *backstory*? First of all, why do we need it? Isn't the "now" of the story enough? Not necessarily. In most cases it's impossible to avoid.

If you just drop it in like yesterday's pizza, you're headed for problems. Remember: Thoughtful. Purposeful. Deliberate. Keep that in mind when dealing with elements like backstory. You never want to be gratuitous (with anything!) but it's very tempting and also a bit problematic with backstory.

But if it happened before your story, how do you get it into the "now"? I don't want to encourage you to do anything gratuitous, but there are many ways to do it and even the best movies manage to smuggle it in in inventive ways. Sometimes you can deal with it in a pretty simple manner, like just tell it. But be clever and above all, be dramatic.

First thing you need is to know the backstory you're trying to include. This can come from your character bio that you wrote. It can also come from a moment in which you are defining your character's major problem, deficit, and pathology. How did he/she get that way? What were the events in this character's fictional life that brought him/her to the point of your present story?

One of the most famous backstories of course is in *Moby Dick*.

Since the loss of his leg (and his self-esteem), Captain Ahab has been obsessed with killing the eponymous great white whale. This is ingenious (Melville was brilliant). Ahab has one leg and when our narrator (see below!) asks, he's told about the tragedy. There's your backstory; it's information for the character *and* the audience.

This goes into the category of "previous scars and injuries" that can be very readily (and visually!) displayed.

Certainly *Chinatown* gets the "E-Z Backstory" award. We get a good taste of it when Gittes goes out to a reservoir to pick up more information on the key murder at the opening of the story.

Who should he run into but his old partner Lou Escobar (Perry Lopez). Here we get a conversation about the deep dark past cloaked as a discussion of lighting matches and two diverging careers. It's the first taste we get of Gittes' past as a police officer and the way he is regarded by the guys who stayed on the force. There is a heightened sense of resentment from his former colleagues. We even hear the first mention of "Chinatown" as the setting of their previous lives.

The scene avoids being a dull exposition because of the inherent conflicts between these characters. We are caught up in how they are going to parry with each other. How Escobar pays Gittes a few sarcastic compliments and finally how Escobar is able to reverse the scene upon Gittes' request to talk to Hollis Mulwray — just as they approach the place where the man's dead body is being pulled out of a concrete channel.

Another water-related backstory is in *Jaws*. The three guys are sitting around one night comparing scars. Chief Brody can barely show a shaving cut. Hooper jokingly points to his heart and how his first girlfriend broke it. But then old Quint tells a riveting story of being on the crew of the ship that brought the atom bombs to Okinawa and how on its return journey was blown out of the water. It's a mesmerizing tale of death and tragedy as the last floating survivors are eaten one at a time by sharks. By the end not only are Brody and Hooper humbled, but Quint also says, "I'll never put on a life jacket again."

This is not just good backstory — it's a masterful way to present it. This is a combined effort of director Steven Spielberg, screenwriter Carl Gottlieb, and John Milius, a screenwriter and script doctor who is credited with contributing this powerful monologue.

In *The Verdict*, with a screenplay by Pulitzer Prize–winner David Mamet (from a strong and decent novel by Barry Reed), and directed by the master Sidney Lumet, there is a long list of things we need to know about our main character that occurred long before the story has begun.

First of all, Frank Galvin (Paul Newman) an ambulance-chasing attorney, is a terrible drunk. A fall-down lush who spends most of his days playing pinball down at the local tavern. But how did he get that way? What made him so miserable? And just how much of a bum is he?

This is very simply presented during Act I of the story. As he takes on a medical malpractice lawsuit against a Catholic hospital, our POV is suddenly shifted (but not too abruptly) to the offices of the archdiocese, where a bishop is informed about Galvin's record. Pretty convenient, eh? If the scene were set simply to recite this character's CV, then I would object. But the scene also shows the bishop's own trepidations regarding the suit. He also states that the archdiocese doesn't want this kind of attention. He does not want the case to go to trial. His legal advisor reassures him that they would win, but first he gives a short recap of Galvin's career history. It's a pretty sad story. This is where he's called "an ambulance chaser."

One of the most economical presentations of backstory is in *Being John Malkovich*.

Our hero, puppeteer Craig Schwartz (John Cusack), performs his odd puppet works on street corners in Manhattan. This alone stands as significant backstory. He's obviously fallen to the bottom of his expectations.

The kind of puppet show he's doing portrays the forbidden medieval love affair of "Abelard and Heloise." Schwartz's puppets reenact a scene with astounding sexuality, rubbing their marionette bodies against a stone wall in unison.

But wouldn't you know it, there's a little girl watching, standing with her father. In a moment, the sexual activity of the puppets reaches (yes!) a climax, just as the father turns around to see it and *wham!* slams Schwartz a good one right in the kisser!

The very next cut is Schwartz walking into his wife's pet store where she greets him sympathetically with "Oh honey! Not again!"

What an efficient use of backstory and movie time. In just an instant, we get his past along with his present.

Another Charlie Kaufman film, *Adaptation,* shows the comic struggles of Charlie Kaufman (Nicolas Cage) to adapt a book, *The Orchid Thief,* into a movie. He is beset not by his own misery, neurosis, and insecurity, but also by his overconfident twin brother Donald (also Nicolas Cage).

In one scene Donald remarks how "Mom is paying for the seminar" and " . . . I pitched mom. She loved my . . . telling of my story to her. She said 'it's like *Silence of the Lambs* meets *Psycho.*'"

We immediately feel Charlie's strange oedipal pangs of jealousy with his twin brother. Later references to their mother (whom we never see) all refer to her as a champion of Donald. This is valid backstory because it reinforces an off-screen relationship that both characters have with their mother. One feels creepily supported, the other completely rejected. This is backstory that reinforces character deficit.

If you can bring in a powerful offstage relationship or off-screen experience, this can work to reinforce backstory. The word *always* can be very powerful in the now when used to describe any character's past behavior. The word *never* is pretty handy too.

Once again, in *Chinatown* in Act III, when Gittes is just about to pull the wool over the eyes of Escobar, the police lieutenant looks at him like a disappointed parent and says, "You never learn, do you, Jake?"

Sometimes the broken promises of one character to another can be very powerful. In how many bank robbery movies do we hear "But you promised you'd give it up; that this was the last job"? Promises made before the start of your story can be used as evidence against your character's integrity in the "now" story.

If you know your character's backstory, it's because you've devised a past that is necessary to the present of your story. If your character is trying to do the right thing, it's usually because he/she failed at it before. If your character is going to finally stand up to a bully, it's because he was a coward in the past.

Whatever the reason, your backstory inclusion cannot be put there for the audience. It must be put there for the characters.

"That's Me Talking, In Case You Didn't Recognize Me . . . ": Voiceover Dos & Don'ts

In the autobiographical *Adaptation* (written and directed by Charlie Kaufman) Nicolas Cage (playing Kaufman), desperate to finish his script, has swallowed the last of his pride and now sits in the audience of the famous screenwriting seminar conducted by Robert McKee (played in perfect facsimile by Brian Cox). In voiceover, used generously throughout the movie, we listen to Kaufman's familiar agony and ambivalence about attending such a seminar and his unending struggle to write his screenplay: "I should leave here right now. I'll start over . . . I need to face this project head on and —" at which point his thoughts are abruptly cut off by McKee who screams: " — and God help you if you use voiceover! God f'ing help you! It's flaccid, sloppy writing. Any idiot can write voiceover narration to explain the thoughts of a character. You must present the internal conflicts of your character in image, in symbol. Film is a medium of movement and image."

How right he is! But wait a second, don't we use voiceover all the time? So the question really is when to use voiceover and when not to use voiceover and, most importantly, how to use it well.

My basic thumbnail rules of voiceover are simple:

1. **Don't tell us what we're seeing.** In those old (not so great) 1950s detective movies we'll listen to a description of what we're watching as our detective makes a few stops, asks a few muted characters a few questions, and then settles into a full scene with dialogue. These types of sequences were designed purely to save screen time and money.
2. **Don't tell us what we just saw.** (see above)
3. **Don't tell us what we're about to see.** These are deadly. You will make a character actually say what he/she is going to do next.

If you want to talk through or explain the story, then write a radio script.

This brings us to the real challenge. When faced with the use of voiceover, ask this question right away: "Can what I am 'telling' in the voiceover be 'shown'?"

That's right: "Tell or Show?" That is the big question.

My option is always to try to show rather than tell. It's what we're all about. Then of course there are many instances where a voiceover can make a sound (forgive the pun!) contribution to your story.

In Orson Welles' *The Lady from Shanghai* our hero, a doltish Irish adventurer, narrates this story of lust, greed, intrigue, and murder. But the entire time, he's always telling us, "I'm an idiot and this is what happens to an idiot." For the most part the voiceover presents us with the character's own ironic, weak approach to his life choices.

In *Adaptation* Kaufman is telling us every petty emotion and fantasy that's going on in the head of "Him," the fictionalized Kaufman portrayed by Nicolas Cage. But not only is this voiceover hilarious, it is also a deep look inside the mind of a man with no self-esteem; who believes the entire world is set against him and who lives in the expectation of constant disappointment. While he is self-judging, he makes us laugh every time he says, "I'll try. I'll try . . . oh never mind, what's the use in trying." The voiceover provides its own sense of character using the exaggerated personality of a man who refuses to be happy.

Throughout *Adaptation,* the wall-to-wall voiceover is not describing what we're seeing, but only what the character is feeling. The voiceover is mostly about his inner thoughts and struggle with writing an un-writable screenplay. The action of the story plays out with all the proper underpinnings of a good story and the voiceover underscores not only the hopelessness of the struggle, but our protagonist's personal hopelessness as well. But it never talks about what we see. In fact, only when there are quotes from the original book *The Orchid Thief* by Susan Orlean do we hear Meryl Streep's voiceover simply reading from the book. This of course is Kaufman's imagined "hearing" of the book as he reads through it.

In another extreme, let's look at the films of Terrence Malick. Here is a filmmaker who worships the visual world of film and invites us to take this journey with him. His first film, *Badlands,* featured the voiceover of the female character (Sissy Spacek) a teenager lured onto a murder rampage by a James Dean–handsome Martin Sheen. But her voiceover is as innocent as what you would find in a lovesick teenager's private diary. It never looks at the horrifying deeds, never explains who she is or what is happening on screen. It's a real study in what I call the *dissociated voiceover.* The very use of it, in counterpoint to the events, gives us a wide range of character. This type of use also underscores a character's own deep denial of the tragic events he/she experiences in the story. Its neutrality is nothing less than haunting and makes the story even more distressing and more dramatic.

Malick made another movie a few years later, *Days of Heaven,* in which he uses the voiceover of another young girl, the preadolescent sister of the main character (played with a streetwise snap by Linda Manz). It also has a quasi-innocence; a haunting detachment that really works to support another tragic story of love and murder.

It would be about twenty years before Malick would make another film, *The Thin Red Line*, a harrowing look at World War II in the Pacific. The film is replete with voiceovers, throwaway characters, random POV switches, and elliptical moments. It takes some adjustment, but once you're along for the ride, it's worth it. There is the riveting tension of the battle scenes contrasted with the sensual visuals of the fauna and flora of the South Pacific plus the poetic journeys into the minds of the varied characters through its voiceovers. In my opinion it's a film that perfectly captures the fear, madness, and loneliness of war. Without its unique style, it would not be the masterpiece I believe that it is. Once again, a detached, otherworldly, and utterly poetic voiceover style makes this experience unique and very compelling. At the same time, it violates almost all of the structural character elements I've asked you to follow in this book. A good example of a filmmaker who plays solely by his own rules. Let's remember, there was a twenty-year gap between his second and third movies.

In his subsequent recent films Malick uses an almost identical technique — an elliptical, detached voiceover that may or may not match what we are seeing. It is almost as if he made the visuals, then created the voiceover in an utterly unrelated manner and then put them together to create this hybrid experience. It's not necessarily easy to understand, but at times it is hypnotic and, I feel, very engaging and dramatic.

Election probably contains the most daring and most successful use of voiceover. The script by Jim Taylor and Alexander Payne (based on the Tom Perotta novel) tells the story of a high school election. But the screenwriters decided to use four different voiceovers. On the face of it you would think that I (and Robert McKee) would be apoplectic. On the contrary, it is not only successful but helps define what I feel is the perfect use of voiceover.

Fundamentally, as this bleakly hilarious story unfolds, it becomes apparent — à la *Rashomon* — that getting to the actual "truth" of what happened at Carver High will be a struggle, not only for us, but also for our characters. What we finally discover is that everybody is lying. The cleverly orchestrated "testimony" through voiceover is in direct contrast to the unfolding events. Not only are the events and character actions completely engaging, but we are also riveted by this weird denial that each character expresses.

In the end, we are left with a story about facing the truth featuring characters who cannot face the truth. This is a deep irony and it is deeply comic.

So what can we say about voiceover?

```
                ME (VO)
     Whatever I say right now better not be
     about what we're watching. It shouldn't
     underscore or relate to what's on
     screen, but instead convey a counter-
     point, even a direct opposite to the
     action that we see. It can even be
     a poetic or stylized text that works
     in direct contrast to the onscreen
     action.
```

"Just Listen . . . ": Monologues

I have this strange little thing I call the *chunk-o-meter*. Filmmakers and screenwriters understand this. It's when, before actually reading a script, you simply look at it, quickly skimming the arrangement of text on the pages. Then suddenly — your eye is slammed with huge chunks of text. These are long, unbroken paragraphs of description and/or long passages of one character's dialogue.

Now hang on. If your character needs to talk, then he/she should talk. If your character needs to talk a lot and all at one time, we call that a *monologue*. A monologue is a choice you will need to make and you will need to be thoughtful about it.

First of all, a *deus ex machina* is always delivered in a monologue at the end of a (bad) movie in order to summarize everything in an overcomplicated plot that was poorly conceived. So don't do that (I know, this never occurred to you . . . I'm talking to those screenwriters who are looking for an easy out for their story).

Second, a long passage of dialogue, spoken by one character, is usually spoken to another. Otherwise you'll have a soliloquy. While these are very dramatic — "To be or not to be . . . that is the question" — they are also rarely of practical use in modern films. This is because most films take place in a reality where the characters do not acknowledge the audience, except in a funny way, as when they do that rare thing of "breaking the fourth wall" and actually address the camera. I don't know about you, even though you will catch me talking to myself, I never believe it on screen, except as weak storytelling.

The idea of a character talking to him- or herself for a half page is not normally acceptable. We just don't believe it. Another problem is that for the most part nothing is actually happening while this character drones on, probably only revealing feelings that can be expressed as action if the writer only used a little more imagination.

So, just as thoughtful as you are with your entire story and script elements, you are going to be with the spoken monologue.

The first and best example that leaps to mind is from the wonderful Peter Bogdanovich film *Paper Moon*. The screenplay is by the veteran Alvin Sargent, based on the Joe David Brown novel.

On this journey through the Depression Era Midwest Dust Bowl, Ryan O'Neal as a con artist, Moze, is stuck with transporting an eight-year-old orphan girl, Addie (played by his real-life daughter Tatum) to her aunt in faraway Missouri. Also, right away there is the vague probability that Moze just might be Addie's illegitimate father.

During this cross-country juggernaut, the little girl falls in with Moze, becoming an increasingly indispensable partner. These two form a unique conflict-ridden relationship as con artist partners, using a variety of scams to fleece unsuspecting people along the way.

But Moze is a man and he meets Miss Trixie Delight, a country floozy of the highest order played by the incomparable Madeline Kahn. A rivalry grows between Trixie and Addie until it comes to a head after a hillside picnic as Addie adamantly refuses to get back in the car.

This masterful monologue is a study in thoughtful writing. But it's two pages long! And yet we are completely absorbed in the action of the scene. This is one of the first rules of long passages of dialogue — they must have a real action in the scene. A monologue cannot simply explain story elements or reveal plot.

Set on a hillside on a remote side road, Trixie needs to persuade Addie to get in the car primarily because she has to pee. So right away, we have a very simple motivation for one of the characters. But little Addie also knows that she has complete control over the situation. The contest appears to be "who will ride in the front seat of the car." But as this two-page monologue unfolds it becomes first pleading and cajoling, then bribery and finally confession.

What is most ingenious about this scene is that it justifies the monologue because little Addie is completely silent throughout. She understands the power of her silence and uses it to make Miss Trixie more and more uncomfortable, angrier and weaker, all without uttering a single word.

Each section has been thoughtfully and dramatically conceived to bring out some form of emotion in Miss Trixie.

The monologue is clearly divided into three parts. In the first "act" of this monologue, Miss Trixie offers Addie a coloring book. It's instantly obvious to Miss Trixie that this kid is no "kid."

In the second part, Miss Trixie offers to share the secrets of womanhood, beauty, and attracting men. Being reasonably sure of herself, Miss Trixie ends this part with " . . . but right now you're gonna pick your little ass up and you're gonna drop it in the backseat and you're gonna cut out the crap, you understand?"

Silence . . . from little Addie, who stares at her with eyes that look like little spikes. Unmoved. Immovable.

The next and final section begins with "You're gonna ruin it, ain't ya?" And what follows is the most moving and pathetic autobiography of a woman who knows she has no hope, except jumping in bed with the next man and the next and the . . .

What began with a parental demand has now ended with a pathetic pleading and a final sense of camaraderie that was not present at the beginning. Change.

The actual length of the monologue is determined by Addie's lack of response. Until she responds, it ain't over. So Miss Trixie is forced to continue until some outcome is achieved.

Addie is actually moved and satisfied. She's gotten from Miss Trixie what she wants — surrender — and without firing a shot or speaking a word of dialogue. So this is a "true" monologue that is also a wonderful scene containing a deep action and a dramatic outcome. The story of this scene is not told, it *happens*, through dynamic dramatic action.

You will probably remember your favorite movie monologue as a great speech. The end of Spielberg's *Lincoln.* Capra's *Mr. Smith Goes to Washington* when Jimmy Stewart virtually begs an indifferent Senate floor for justice and democracy. The scene and the monologue are nothing less than a metaphorical plea from the American people. In both instances we expect speeches. This is part of their profession.

One of my favorites in this category comes at the end of *The Verdict.* Frank Galvin (Paul Newman), at the end of his case, has exhausted all possibilities. Not only has he rebuilt the case against impossible odds, but he has — at least technically — presented all the evidence necessary to win the case. In addition, he has journeyed through an ordeal of love and betrayal that has left him feeling completely defeated.

The story is telling us that you can't expect justice from the justice system.

And so, by the time he is called to do his summation, he offers a quiet, dignified plea to the jury to "see in themselves what is right."

First, let's look at the circumstances of this monologue. A final summation by any attorney is in every way a dramatic monologue. Therefore, as a writer, there is realistic license to use it. There are no issues regarding plausibility. Unlike Miss Trixie's monologue, this is not dependent on the emotional moment; it is permissible because of the circumstances of this world.

Galvin has proven his case. But because of the accepted cronyism of the court, evidence has been denied and stricken from the record (but not from the jurors' minds). Also, because Galvin had refused a customary settlement at the outset, he has pissed off everybody. Therefore, even in court, he's not going to get a fair shake. He'll have to fight his way out. In this monologue, he's left to simply plead for justice.

He begins: "You know, so much of the time we're lost. We say 'Please, God, tell us what is right.'"

This opening is in fact the story of this movie and the story of Galvin's own life. As we go a few steps into this eloquent monologue, we hear Galvin tell his own story: "There is no justice. The rich win, the poor are powerless . . . We become tired of hearing people lie. After all we become dead; a little dead. We start thinking of ourselves as victims."

This is Galvin's assessment of *himself* from the beginning of the story. He goes on not only to describe the conflict and difficulty of granting justice but of how religion grants us the faith that "we must only believe in ourselves."

How true. Galvin's journey has been about belief in himself — as both a loser and a winner.

Finally, he says, "I believe that there is justice in our hearts." And he sits slowly back into his chair, exhausted and hopeless. His reward is that he went the distance for something he truly believed in for the first time in his life. This is a powerful story summarized in this powerful moment of this character's life. Everything he knows, believes, and *is* depends on the verdict.

Dramatic circumstances are a good time for a rousing call to battle. Great monologues that galvanize other characters into action are very handy.

One of the best is from David Mamet's movie adaptation of his award-winning play *Glengarry Glen Ross*. The best thing about this monologue is that it is not adapted from the original stage play. It was written expressly for the movie to tie down some structural elements. The play barely had an inciting incident or a call to action. However, Mamet recognized the need for these elements in crafting the screenplay. He created one of the most memorable screen monologues in movie history performed with ruthless precision (and humor) by budding star Alec Baldwin.

In a seven-minute scene where Baldwin speaks 90% of the dialogue to a captive audience of hapless real estate salesmen, Baldwin's unnamed character makes things really clear from the very start:

> "The good news is — you're fired. The
> bad news is you've got, all you got,
> just one week to regain your jobs,
> starting tonight. (PAUSE) Oh, have I
> got your attention now?"

Yes, he certainly does. Mamet does not spare the outrage and selected tool of Baldwin's choice — utter humiliation. He starts out with making one thing clear, which he demonstrates to Jack Lemmon, playing the oldest salesman in the scene, Shelley Levene.

> "Put that coffee down!! Coffee's for
> closers only. Do you think I'm f***ing
> with you? I am not f***ing with you.
> I'm here from downtown. I'm here

```
from Mitch and Murray. And I'm here
on a mission of mercy. Your name's
Levene? . . . You call yourself a
salesman, you son of a bitch?"
```

We're off and running. We understand two elements instantly: 1) Baldwin has nothing but disdain for these men and 2) these men have no self-esteem left. Baldwin is here to spiritually eviscerate them without mercy. He goes on to sweeten the offer:

```
" . . . we're adding a little some-
thing to this month's sales contest. As
you all know, first prize is a Cadillac
Eldorado. Anyone want to see second
prize? Second prize's a set of steak
knives. Third prize is you're fired. You
get the picture? You're laughing now?"
```

No mistaking this character's mission, personality, or character traits. All is laid out without compromise.

With each segment of this monologue Baldwin escalates the stakes until by the climax he is hanging a pair of brass globes over his crotch and says, "You know what you need to sell real estate? It takes brass balls to sell real estate."

The absurdity and the brutality of this statement give this monologue its singular dramatic value. It also serves as both the inciting incident as well as the call to action for these characters. After he's finished, he leaves the office and the story permanently. He's done his work and like a maniacal Johnny Appleseed, he'll "go forth and do likewise" somewhere else, wherever Mitch and Murray send him.

This monologue is utterly practical and realistic. You don't need to know anything about real estate to understand that these men are on their last legs and this "mission of mercy" is exactly that, to put these dying animals out of their misery. This is brutal, honest, and in many ways funny writing at its best.

These types of "public address" monologues are probably the easiest to justify in terms of circumstance and plausibility. Lawyers need to summarize. Politicians and leaders need to make speeches. CEOs need to make important announcements. Generals need to rouse the troops.

For the latter I would recommend *Patton* with a screenplay by Francis Ford Coppola. The movie begins and ends with Patton himself standing in front of the largest American flag imaginable, giving his version of history.

In Kenneth Branagh's exquisite screen version of Shakespeare's *Henry V*, Branagh, as the young king who must defend a puny England, gives one of Shakespeare's most famous monologues to rouse his rag-tag troops to put their lives on the line for their country. Remember, he does this because he has no choice. He hears dissent and hopelessness circulating among his men. He must make a stand to persuade these frightened men, about to go into battle against France's formidable, larger, and better-armed troops:

```
"From this day to the ending of the
world,
But we in it shall be remembered —
We few, we happy few, we band of
brothers;
For he to-day that sheds his blood
with me
Shall be my brother; be he ne'er so
vile."
```

The king is offering his brotherhood to whosoever will stand with him to save the country. Nothing less is at stake but the life of the nation and if we do not fight now, we will perish.

Notice in all of these examples the stakes that were involved in each scene. For Miss Trixie, her very survival in a hapless life. For Galvin, if he loses this case, that's it. He's probably never going to practice law again. For Blake (Baldwin) it is to shake these losers out of themselves and make them get out there and sell. And for young King Henry V, he must at all costs save his country. He must rouse his men to go forth, put their lives on the line and win.

When using the monologue, make sure you have proper motivation for your character and make sure this extended piece of dialogue has a purpose and plausibility given the circumstance. Don't give your character a bunch of things to explain, even if it's to another character. This isn't very natural. The monologue is a work of art unto itself. Remember, this is not a play. Your character can't simply stand there and talk unless there is enough drama and reality to cause your monologue.

"Whose 'Now' Is It Anyway?" — Time and When to Mess with It

Like no other medium, movies can violate, play with, shift, disregard, scramble, and (sometimes) abuse time. Even in stage plays, you might be able to fragment time, but that would mean offering some sort of visual cue so that the audience doesn't get lost.

In film, you can construct a flashback to go back twenty years. You cut — and there you are! Complete with vintage clothing, cars, and setting. Or flash-forward to a made-up future. Wherever you go in time in your movie, instantly, there you are. Sculpture, theater, painting, music, dance, opera, and photography cannot do this.

But this can be abused and overused. As in everything else I've asked of you, I hope you will devote enough thought and deliberation if you should decide to mess around with time.

This is a kick for me because when we're watching a movie we're not experiencing "normal" time in any way. Time is already compressed. We're looking at an experience that could span a day, a few days, or a lifetime in a matter of the usual two hours. We can only experience the now of our film story. Anything "other" is some kind of manipulation of our notion of "normal" time.

So whatever time we experience it's "story time" and has only the most minimal connection to any sort of real time. Yet, we can be disoriented if we can't pin our brains on some sort of time order for a given film.

Let's start with one of the most striking and simplest examples, Christopher Nolan's second feature film, *Memento.*

This is an easy one. Yes, it's a sensational use of "backward" story-telling, something pretty rare. One of the few times it was attempted before was the 1983 adaptation of Harold Pinter's British play *Betrayal.* But unlike *Memento,* the scenes were presented in individual normal-time chunks working backward from the outcome of a love triangle to its beginnings.

In *Memento* our hero's journey appears to start at its end and then works its way back to its beginning, but in fragments of the present that must be connected by the hero (and us). Of course the genius of Nolan's structure is that the story still has a beginning, middle, and end, but only for the other characters and the audience.

There's a strong justification for the use of this technique. The main character is afflicted with a neurological disorder that causes severe short-term memory loss. We experience time in the same way as our main character. Confusing at first, but once we settle into it, we're along for the ride. It's easily one of the most creative uses of time in movie history. It's also a film noir/detective story, so we are left with the same confusion as our hero as he tries to piece together his past . . . which may or may not actually exist.

In Nolan's first feature, *Following,* he appears to fracture time simply to make the story more interesting.

From the moment *Following* begins, its time is fractured. It opens with a teaser using a scene from the very end of the story. The hero is recounting his tale to someone else, but who? A cop, maybe? Not something we learn until much later.

But after *Following* I can only say that the ordinary was simply made more interesting. Yes, this can be a justification, especially when a filmmaker is in his early years.

Nolan simply wants to play with the limits of time and he includes us in the game. He wants us to understand the story in a fragmented manner. For a first feature it is a great attempt at doing something different just for the sake of elevating the genre. Then Nolan does something thoroughly unique. He takes a little piece of Act I, a piece of Act II, and another scene or sequence from Act III and puts them together into these little packages in that I-II-III order. These packages are separated by a few seconds of black, then they recycle.

What happens is that each segment literally consumes the next. Funny, but once we get used to it, we are always sure of where we are throughout the film. This is because Nolan packages it so neatly and in order, over and over, until once we learn the "code," we're completely comfortable. Our first thrill is a slight disorientation. Next, we try to crack the code. And finally, once we've cracked it, we're along for the ride. An otherwise ordinary low-budget film noir is raised up a rung or two into a metaphysical hybrid.

Now we can move to the obvious: time machine movies. *The Time Machine* (1960), *Hot Tub Time Machine*, *Run Lola Run*, *Groundhog Day*, and *Looper*. All of these have time travel or time distortion as part of their story.

The Time Machine (1960) is classic science fiction, adapted from the 1895 H. G. Welles classic. It is a classic not simply because it is old, but because like all great sci-fi, it's about *today*.

The protagonist in *The Time Machine* is a genius scientist and inventor. He perfects his time travel machine and goes forward in time. He discovers that the world will be destroyed by global war and then be reborn as a split society. Above ground are the Eloi, a delicate and beautiful race who frolic and eat all day. Our scientist soon falls in love with Mina, a most beautiful girl. He soon discovers a dark side to this idyllic society. Every day an air-raid siren is sounded and the Eloi go into a trance and march en masse down underground to serve as slaves and food for the Morlocks, a breed of underground monster who actually dominate this world.

There's no great gimmick here. Our hero travels forward in time, learns what the world will be like, finds love, and in the end it appears that he will never return to his present time.

Hot Tub Time Machine is similar, but it is a romantic comedy. In this story our hero, played by John Cusack, has blown a romantic opportunity and through the sheer will of wishing for it, he can use an ordinary hot tub as a time machine. In the course of the story and over several attempts to remake his present, he finally succeeds and gets the girl he should have been with all along. Phew! Once again, a time machine can be a vehicle for finding love. The value here is "Take your opportunity when you can — you never know if you'll have another chance."

Run Lola Run simply proposes a world where our heroine, Lola (Franka Potente) has three attempts at her goal in three slightly different sequences of events. What's the justification? None. I love this movie for that reason alone (not to mention the fact that it's just wonderful). Filmmaker Tom Tykwer simply does it. He doesn't ask our permission. He doesn't set up a mystical time warp or future time travel idea. Lola does not have a brain condition. He simply starts the movie and then restarts it twice more in a loop, but with the slightest change of physical events.

Groundhog Day does something entirely unique. Our hero is a dick played by Bill Murray (as only he can play one!). This is a guy who needs severe changing. He's in dire need of some kind of spiritual wake-up call. It comes in the form of one day, February 2, repeated over and over. What's great about this story is that we glide along with this character as he soon discovers and then believes what is happening to time. Then we are along for the ride when he gets hip to how to use it! Similar to both *The Time Machine* and *Hot Tub*.

Like *Memento*, *Groundhog Day* uses this time gimmick as an active metaphor for our hero's state of being. He is stuck, really stuck in his life because he's not growing, not changing. Screenwriters Harold Ramis and Danny Rubin use this value in the story and are able to match it to the journey of our hero. What happens when the same day suddenly starts repeating and now you have all this time to do things that you never did before?

There's a really terrific comic irony here: this limitation to a single day, lived over and over, ultimately provides our hero with more, rather than less, opportunity to start to make great changes to his life. By the end he's earned his normal time back.

One may ask: Why do we so easily believe this? It's simple: the story takes us along into an alternate reality of time repetition because this is the state of the character's being. He's stuck in a psychic loop. More importantly, there's no time machine or device. How come we believe it so strongly?

Finally, in *Looper* we're treated to the ultimate in the "Zombie Rules" of time travel. Isn't it funny how strictly we tend to obey and believe in these quirky, made-up rules?

Looper actually adheres very strictly to this rule and uses it to show the personal crisis it can create. There's a choice of whether to murder yourself or not! What's great about this movie is that writer-director Rian Johnson sets up a set of circumstances and plot points that make this believable and active, much like *Memento*.

The first level of this concept is that time travel, although possible, is illegal. It is only used by criminals in the future, so we're never shown a device or how it actually works. This is a great notion: if you can't build a time machine, then don't! The film really pulls off a great stunt of settling on the characters' struggles rather than the trivialities of the Zombie Rules. We learn enough and we know enough as the story unfolds to be with it the whole way.

Fundamentally, if you're going to play with time or time travel, don't treat it like a toy. Take it seriously and your audience will not be lost. But if you're doing it to simply create a gimmick to build interest, it's going to boomerang on you. Always make it a solid part of your character's story.

Plants and Payoffs

Screenwriting by its very nature is the arrangement of things. How you lay things out in a screenplay is like the seating plan at a state dinner. Everything must be done with great care.

It is amazing how astute your audience can be. While some cannot remember what they did two hours before they came to the movies, by the end of your movie, they can and will remember some event, phrase, or object that was planted at the beginning. This is something you did deliberately.

Something like "Rosebud . . . " coupled with an image of a child's snow scene clutched in the hand of a dying man. It's one of the greatest payoffs in movie history. It was, in my opinion, Orson Welles' tribute to how we can use image and idea to convey an important and compelling human value.

Plants and payoffs have been used in movies since the beginning. One can say that they are unique to movies, although in ancient Greek and Roman comedies lovers might find out they are actually brother and sister when they discover they wear the same ring. It can be compared to the musical term *leitmotif*, a steadily recurring figure of melody. It provides a repeating anchor that grabs the listener's attention and sends them into the next movement. Here is where movies and music are highly comparable.

Movies have somewhat of a corner on the market for plants and payoffs. In many ways, some movies are built entirely of plants and payoffs.

In *Three Days of the Condor*, during the opening sequence, we are treated to a close-up of a gun in the drawer of the receptionist. A few minutes later, as Robert Redford's character is confronted with the murder of everyone in his office, he grabs the gun. But as you watch the scene, it would be a good bet that you are saying to yourself: "The gun! Get the gun in the drawer!" — and of course he does.

In one sense this is why they are called *payoffs*. They are not only a part of the subtly planted props of the story, but also pay off for the audience with a feeling of satisfaction; a "closing of the loop" as it were.

In *Maria Full of Grace,* Maria's pregnancy is the plant that keeps paying off — regardless of the fact that it is also her biggest problem.

At the very opening she beckons Juan to join her on the roof, saying, "I have something to tell you." When she vomits on the flowers, this is her morning sickness. The pregnancy is also driving her to take more responsibility.

Later at US Customs, it saves her because she cannot be x-rayed.

Then, in the Queens Hispanic neighborhood, she realizes she should find out about the state of her fetus. She gets a sonogram and a printout photo.

In the final scenes of the film, while riding in a taxi, she pulls out the sonogram and an appointment card for a checkup. Within the next few minutes this will pay off in her final decision to stay in the US and not return to Colombia. This is an elegant plant with a deeply compelling payoff.

Spielberg and Lucas are great fans of plants and payoffs.

In *Raiders of the Lost Ark* Indiana Jones' fear of snakes is presented in the opening moments of the film. Later, he will have to confront his greatest fear in order to survive.

Jaws is another hotbed of plants and payoffs. First, Sheriff Brody has a morbid fear of the water. He will have to confront this fear in order to defeat the shark and survive. When they are preparing the boat, Brody, having seldom been on the water, pulls a rope and accidentally causes the oxygen tanks to crash to the deck. Quint and Hooper freak out explaining the danger of the tanks exploding. "Jeesh!" Of course later, those tanks are going to save Brody's life. In one instant Brody has been given important information and information has been smuggled to the audience. A great example of "information for the characters (. . . and we know the audience is eavesdropping!)."

A very dramatic plant in *Silver Linings Playbook* is the letter that Tiffany has claimed she has delivered to Pat's wife. Of course she hasn't and when this is revealed, it is the great emotionally wrenching moment that almost destroys their new relationship.

In *Up in the Air* it is Jack's (George Clooney) greatest hope to accrue one million flyer miles. This number trails the story from the beginning to the end. The great moment arrives finally near Act III. But at this point Jack has experienced an amazing disappointment and he is absolutely unable to enjoy it. In fact, in a grand gesture of love and recognition, he gives away the mileage to his sister and her new husband to take their around-the-world dream honeymoon. This plant is used with terrific irony. It is also the "false goal" that defines this character's shallow and lonely life.

Going back to classic Hollywood, one of my favorite payoffs is in *Casablanca*.

At the opening of the film, we learn Rick's precarious relationship with the highly corruptible police chief, Renaud. A trumped up "bust" at Rick's Café is accompanied by Renaud's famous line, "Round up the usual suspects." At this moment it's frustrating for Rick because it is part of his grudging and cynical acceptance of the duplicitous world of an occupied city and its corrupt police force. Although we know he believes in justice, he lives in a world where none really exists.

Yet later, at the climax of the film, moments after Rick has shot and killed the villainous Nazi Major Strasser, a party of police arrives. There is a bracing moment when we cut from Renaud to Rick — what will he tell them? And back to Renaud as he says, "Round up the usual suspects."

Not only is this an amazing payoff, but it is also a great reversal of the character, a twist of the moment. It takes a potentially tragic

ending and turns it upside down into a stirring and heroic denouement. It's also the height of Hollywood wit, something that is sadly
missing from so many movies these days.

Your plant can be for simple information for the character (*Jaws*)
or the ticking time bomb in *Condor*. The plant in *Up in the Air* reveals
the disappointing values of our hero that must — and ultimately do
— change. In *Casablanca* the same simple wisecrack, which earlier
in the film is seen as a negative and corrupt, finally saves the day.

The Sidekick, the Mentor, the Student, and All Those Other Types of Characters

Believe it or not knowing what type of character you are creating will
help you achieve a kind of balance in your story. I don't mean what
kind of person your character is, like "smart" or "funny" or "bossy"
or "conservative." I mean how this type of character fits into your
story.

In *Of Mice and Men* we clearly see the difference between the
two main characters. George, a skillful and seemingly smart guy,
can't change his relationship with Lenny, the big, lovable, intellectually challenged human time bomb. Nice arrangement of contrasts
between the two.

Understanding and supporting these differences helps you bring
clarity to your story. Let's be honest, if Robin were the same age as
Batman or was just as skilled or had the same leadership qualities, it
wouldn't be "Batman and Robin" it would be "Batman with Robin"
or, even worse, "Batmanrobin." This is the last thing you want —
characters that aren't clearly differentiated. More importantly, you
want them to serve very specific roles in your story.

In *Dog Day Afternoon* you will find a very similar partnership as
in *Of Mice and Men*. Sonny (Al Pacino) is clearly the leader — the
"brains" of the operation. His partner Sal (John Cazale) is clearly
not. After Sonny has bargained for their escape via jet, he asks Sal
which country he wants to go to. Sal replies, "Wyoming."

This is not only one of the many dark laughs in the story, but also a revelation for Sonny. He never realized how limited Sal's intellect was. This serves the story later as Sal's dependability while holding an automatic machine gun becomes a suspenseful moment. Nobody, including the audience, really knows how far Sal might go if he gets panicked.

I would call these character relationships "George & Lenny." *Of Mice and Men* was the ultimate "buddy" story of its generation. It is an inspiration and template for many films that have followed.

This is the same relationship as Abbott & Costello, Laurel & Hardy, and Martin & Lewis. While neither is actually smart or capable, one of them believes himself to be the smarter. What follows is the kind of conflict that leads to unmitigated comedy.

This is a very stark contrast for stories that depend on the conflicts caused by these types of relationships.

In *Star Wars* you have a very nice variety of character types. Luke, the young hero, is the student to his mentor, Yoda. He is also given what is known as "supernatural aid" by Obi-Wan Kenobi. His "ally antagonist" is Han Solo, a character who shows daring when it's necessary and is always cynical about his mission. He's the "adventurer" and closer to Harrison Ford's later character of Indiana Jones. He is usually seen giving good advice to Luke, whose youthful idealism can lead to danger. Princess Leia is, well, very clearly the "damsel in distress." Of course Darth Vader is the "dark knight"; the absolute villain of villains. *Star Wars* gets almost all of its basic elements from classical mythology such as "King Arthur" and "The Odyssey."

Within this group you not only find strong contrasts but also each one serves to assist our hero with his journey. Each also questions him, cajoles him, criticizes him, shows loyalty to him, and comes up with an idea or two that will save everybody's skin.

In Tarantino's *Django Unchained* we are watching a "mentor-student" relationship. This gives the Act III "All is Lost" moment even more impact when Dr. Schultz is killed. Our feeling is "Now what is Django going to do?" Dr. Schultz mentored and guided Django through every moment of danger. Now he's gone! This blends with a story about personal freedom and true independence. Tarantino has constructed two levels of liberation for Django. The first, to end his slavery. But the second, which I feel is far more dramatic, is his involuntary liberation when Dr. Schultz is killed. Now he must fight for his own freedom! So Tarantino isn't simply using Schultz as a mentor, but also as dramatic linchpin in the high point of the story.

While there may be characters who are called the "sidekick," I feel this term may not convey their true function. I prefer the more academic term, *ally-antagonist*.

Let's remember that your story is designed to antagonize your protagonist. You are writing the story to exert enough pressure on your hero/-ine to make him/her change or come to a profound realization. Therefore every character you place in the path of their journey must function to bug them a little, question their authority, rub a little sand on them — that's how you get that pearl.

In *The Verdict*, Paul Newman's mentor is also his ally-antagonist. Beautifully played by Jack Warden, every scene with Mickey Morrissey is designed to present two sides to him, and in turn, two sides to the conflicted Frank Galvin. It is Morrissey who brings the big case to Frank, but tells his lifelong buddy about his drunken life "I can't take this anymore. This stuff has to change." He goes on to advise, exhort, criticize, warn, obstruct, inspire, save, and ultimately look up to Galvin who was his best student but worst-case scenario. This occurs in practically every scene that these two characters share. He may be at and on Galvin's side, but he's there to cause more distress and/or promote the hero's progress.

The Verdict even has its own damsel in distress in the form of Laura (Charlotte Rampling). At first her "distress" appears to be the same as Galvin's. She also has a seemingly lonely life filled with disappointment. But later, we come to truly understand her self-loathing.

She is finally the worst that a lawyer can be. It's a manifestation of what could happen to Galvin if he doesn't change.

Of course, the antagonists in *The Verdict* come in the form of the opposing legal team, who appear invincible. There is also a judge who will not give Galvin any kind of break and instead uses his courtroom to try to destroy Galvin. And even the family of the plaintiff, a perfectly innocent working-class couple, actually stand in Galvin's way when he decides not to settle with these "monsters" (as they are later called).

Then there are what are known as *impact* characters. This is tricky. These characters may overlap in some regard with those other characters we've already considered, including your antagonist.

Literally, an impact character is one who has a significant impact on your main character. You would be right to say, "Don't all of my characters have an impact on my main character?" The answer of course is "yes." However, you can think of the impact character in a different way.

Let's treat this impact character as a kind of "advance man" for your main character. This impact character has been through a similar journey already or is about to precede your hero. He/she is the "warning label" in everything he/she does.

In *Up in the Air* Ryan Bingham is beset by a journey that makes him confront a) a new approach to his work that may make him obsolete and b) the fact that he falls in love. Screenwriters Ivan Reitman and Sheldon Turner push Ryan's face into both problems by creating the character of Natalie Keener, an ambitious go-getter who is going to bring the corporate downsizing business into the digital age. She has another quality too. She's suffering in her love life. Both of these arcs play out for Natalie and they impact Ryan. Her pain, her ambition, and her dedication. These are all qualities that exactly match those of Ryan.

But she is also hurt by all three and in the end walks away from Ryan's company and the profession. This has a very well-defined impact on the story and on the main character. It is almost as if your shadow gets a few steps ahead of you and is able to give you a momentary preview of your life. Yes, the main character can't apply the brakes in time because of his own inner conflict and the need to maintain the status quo and not change. Your impact character goes into the lion's den just ahead of your protagonist and when your hero hears the screams, there is an impact on his/her resolve and his/her actions.

In *Quiz Show* Charles Van Doren (Ralph Fiennes) is confronted with the choice of becoming a TV quiz show star (with the wealth and celebrity that comes with it) or upholding the grand family tradition of teaching poetry at Columbia University. So which would you choose? Here is where the character's path to satisfaction and the journey are in wonderfully conflicted contrast.

The character of Charles' father Mark Van Doren (an elegant Paul Scofield) appears only four times. However, his impact is very strongly felt. In each scene, he lays down the importance of their family name, reputation, and legacy. The subtle pressure this exerts on Charles is felt deeply by him and reverberates to us as an audience. In the end it is not only Charles' disappointment in himself, but his father's as well that compounds the highly dramatic arc of this sad story. The father stands as the true goal of our character who is, ultimately, not able to reach it.

Similarly, the character of Herbie Stempel (John Turturro) foreshadows for Van Doren what happens when the network eats you up and spits you out. He's the "be careful what you wish for" character.

In *Memento* the movie uses a stylized "off-story flashback" (a "flashaway"?) to tell the story of Sammy Jankis, a diabetic who suffered from the same kind of memory loss as our hero, Leonard. In this side-story we (and Leonard) see and understand the true nature and ultimate danger of his neurological condition. It is presented as almost a tale-told, which is something retrieved from Leonard's scattered long-term memory and retold to himself. The sequences are presented in black and white and take on an almost fairy-tale kind of quality. Here, the Sammy character acts as a warning to our protagonist: you can forget everything, including how to live.

In *Chinatown* Evelyn Mulwray is a good example of an overlap of a damsel in distress and an impact character. While she is not only a victim of the antagonist's evil, she is also striving to do the same thing as Gittes — expose the evil and bring down her father, Noah Cross. As the story progresses, she is the font of information that ultimately reveals Cross' despicable evil. But she is tragically destroyed by it and Gittes' own recognition becomes doubly painful: the victims are extinguished and evil endures.

In *Maria Full of Grace*, Maria's experience with Clara is the impact and pivot that causes Maria to make the final decision to stay in New York. Clara is also a partner in the Act III "All Is Lost" when Maria is caught in a terrible lie about the death of Clara's sister Lucy (the mentor character who gives Maria her "intro" to drug muling). Clara is also pregnant, has also left her native country, and has chosen a new life in the US. It is her touching and beautiful monologue to Maria in the bedroom that plants the seeds for Maria to consider a new life in a new world and shapes Maria's ultimate decision at the end.

The whole idea is not to simply give these characters labels such as protagonist, antagonist, or mentor. It means you have a responsibility to use these characters for real dramatic purposes. Remember: you're a responsible screenwriter. No character left behind.

I recommend that you simply create your story treatment until you recognize these characters as they emerge. These labels should then help you strengthen their function in the story. This adds clarity and story functionality, creating a strong and clear world for your character to travel through.

To Montage or Not Montage

The over 1,250 students who have studied with me know my feelings about the "M" word. Maybe it's a phobia or more like an allergy. Or possibly because I have seen this technique abused so much over the years that I have often felt like starting a movement to get it outlawed. But the problem is, like anything invented for movies, we really do need it.

Originally the word *montage* simply meant the most fundamental act of splicing two different images together. It was the simplest way to describe the dynamic of film. The French have always had a love of movies and a great gift for creating terms that we all use universally: *film noir, genre, denouement,* and *nouvelle vague.*

Later, as Hollywood adopted certain techniques, montage came to mean a sequence that must bridge a large segment of story time in a short sequence. Often, this was mandated when scenes had to be cut and action compressed for the sake of running time. It was sometimes used to cover story and production errors. Montage sequences were often created by film editors and were not called for in scripts. In fact, in the early days of talkies, a montage was a throwback to an earlier silent-era form of film storytelling. Audiences weren't quite ready for subtextual dialogue or the more subtle visual action that came sometime later.

What I'm getting at is: I think it's a crutch. Yet, we all may have the need to use it. My concerned advice to you is to make sure you don't make your movie one montage sequence after another. Not only will it look silly, but also it will lack story integrity.

We all remember the really cheesy montage sequences of the past like calendar pages flipping, opening night sequences, falling into sin, et cetera.

This is what I propose. Since we don't slap a title on the film that reads "Flashback," I recommend the same approach for these montage sequences in your script. Instead of portraying your action as a list of "things" to simply display, why not create a sequence of short actions that accomplish the same thing? And while you're at it, use the three-act structure to build energy. That means your montage sequence has a beginning, middle, and end.

Your montage can be used to show a succession of attempts by the character. For example, say he is trying to charm a love interest. Start with a shot of your hero delivering flowers, then getting the door slammed. The next beat: he's bringing a more elaborate food basket — door slam! In the next, a puppy! Door slam! And in the next, a sailboat. Next shot: the happy couple sailing out to sea, the sun setting on the horizon.

A montage should have a progression and escalation in the same way as your entire story. Think of it as a miniature stand-alone movie that is going to bridge the time between the scene before and the scene after the sequence. But in any case it must get us from one point in time to another.

Perhaps you're attempting to bridge a seasonal gap in time. A character has an experience in summer that is followed by the next scene in winter. But in the interim, you need to communicate his state of mind. This can be done in a quick succession of scenes. But be sure you describe it as real action. You should also use your slug-lines (scene headings) as you would for actual full-length scenes. Be specific about action and mood. This is especially important if you are pushing your character to some kind of climax at the end of the montage.

In *Midnight Cowboy* after Joe Buck (Jon Voight) has been deceived and conned by Ratso (Dustin Hoffman), we watch his grotesque dream sequence where he thinks he sees Ratso everywhere he goes, in the subways and on the streets. But it's only a fantasy (it's in black and white), until the final bit of the sequence when he spots Ratso in a coffee shop (the picture returns to color), then grabs him and almost punches him out. This is a terrific example of montage bridging time, but it is also building up story energy in its own mini-story-within-a-story.

Quiz Show actually does its own spoof of old-fashioned montages when it shows Charles Van Doren repeatedly answering every question correctly then going on to more fame and notoriety. The movie is set in the 1950s and celebrates the period of the movies with this type of montage.

Groundhog Day, which might be considered the time-bridge movie of all time, uses a series of quick scenes to show Bill Murray's repeated time warp. It occurs at a point in the film where he (and we) have grown accustomed to the time warp he's been trapped in. The sequence gets him through a few necessary actions that don't need to be shown in detail, but do need to convey the repetitive nature of his new life as well as his progressive growth.

Whatever you do with a montage, don't put it in as a placeholder. Many novice screenwriters believe they can simply place this in their screenplay:

```
MONTAGE
Joe becomes a drug addict, losing his fam-
ily, losing his home, and ending up in a
crack house.
```

This is actually four separate scenes and locations. I would do it this way:

```
SERIES OF QUICK SCENES:
INT. DRUG DEN - NIGHT
Joe cooks heroin in a spoon. He ties off
with a rubber tourniquet and mainlines a
needle in his arm.

EXT. JOE'S SUBURBAN HOUSE - DAY
Joe watches as his WIFE packs up the car.
A DAUGHTER, 6, in the child seat. The Wife
gets in the car and drives off.
```

```
Joe turns and sees in b.g., a "FOR SALE"
sign on the lawn.

INT. CRACK HOUSE - NIGHT
Joe smoking crack. He gets the first buzz,
closes his eyes, and enjoys the ride.
```

This is a real sequence of events over a long period of time. The next slug would be a full scene showing the results of this experience (which we'll call "hitting bottom").

So don't use a montage as a way to avoid writing the actual scenes and actions. Use it as a way to bridge time and quickly convey the events and actions of your characters. If you do it right, you'll add story energy rather than simply skip over time. Always be certain to look at your proposed montage and ask yourself: "Am I simply compressing a couple of better scenes in the interests of page count? Or can I make these into short scenes that have real impact?"

Yes, There Is a "Rule of Threes" — And It's Not Stupid

Let's cut to the chase. What is it with this *rule of threes*?!

First of all, it's not really a rule-rule. A real rule is something that if not followed, the violator is punished in some way. Doesn't really happen in screenwriting. But as in many proven rules such as "You gotta cut your wood straight" and "No right turn on red" there is a downside to not following it. Most rules were developed simply because people actually needed them, and the rule of threes is no different.

The Latin phrase *omne trium perfectum* means "everything that comes in threes is perfect," or, "every set of three is complete." This conveys the same idea as the rule of threes. It has something to do with how the human mind processes literature, ideas, and a sequence of dramatic events. Just as I've broken down the "three actions of art," so does the rule of threes make us "Stop, look, and listen." Or better yet, "See . . . Recognize . . . Understand."

We see it in other famous phrases and slogans. "Government of the people, by the people, and for the people." "Blood, sweat, and tears" (not the rock band!), *Sex, Lies and Videotape*, and *Planes, Trains and Automobiles.*

Why "three"? It's almost the same principle as three-act structure. You need a beginning in order to set up certain elements. Then you need a middle in order to develop to a point where it is meaningful. And then you need a third piece to pay off this progression of three. A series of three should create a progression in which the tension is created, built up, and finally released. You can do the same thing with elements of a screen story.

In *Adaptation* Charlie Kaufman actually makes great fun of the rule of threes. The twin brother Donald Kaufman's script is entitled "The 3." It's a patently unbelievable story where the protagonist is not only also the victim but the antagonist as well. Donald actually describes a chase scene with all three. This is Kaufman saying, "Sure you can have a rule of threes, this is what happens when you take it too far."

In *Chinatown* Gittes' story of life as a beat cop in the eponymous neighborhood is told three times. First when he meets up with Escobar at the reservoir crime scene. Second when he meets up with Claude Mulvihill, an old crony, and third when he's in bed with Evelyn Mulwray. In each serving of one third, we get only a piece of it. By the end of the sequence (fairly close to the end of Act II), we now have a complete picture of Gittes' personal and professional history and an important clue as to why the movie has its title. It's been delivered in three small packets, each placed in the story in a strategic manner.

Rather than having some kind of sentimental monologue or another character suddenly saying, "Hey — don't I know you from

Chinatown?" this dramatic undercurrent is made more dramatic by the very act of breaking it into three parts. It serves to heighten our interest and intrigue us at the same time.

There are so many great examples of the rule of threes:

- In Dickens' *A Christmas Carol,* Marley's ghost tells Ebenezer Scrooge he will receive visits from three spirits of Christmas past, present, and future.
- In *The Shawshank Redemption,* Red appears before the parole board three times. The first two times are practically identical. But the third instance is different, indicating how Red changed after Andy left.
- In *Run Lola Run* she goes three times through the slightly changed chain of events.

Be thoughtful when using your rule of threes or any of these other gadgets in your tool bag. Be certain that you are using them for a distinct purpose and not simply to get away with lazy storytelling. Remember, you really can't get away with much in a screenplay. Everybody looking at your script is looking for the fundamental integrity of your story. Even if it's raw action like *The Fast and the Furious* or *Pacific Rim.* The audience is looking for the struggle of the main characters.

Chapter 8

OKAY, NOW GO WRITE YOUR SCRIPT!

"Be quiet and ordinary in your life so you may be violent
and original in your work." —Gustav Flaubert

The "Certainty Principle" — You and Your Story

I've given you a lot to do. In show business, as in all art, everything is
in the preparation. What you're about to actually do is write, but not
like a writer sets down to write a novel or a journalist an article or me
with this book. You're not stacking words together. What you will be
doing is translating your ideas, values, and actions into a seeable and
performable document, the script.

THE IDEA

You've thought up some kind of idea. In order to move to the next
step, just write down, "There's this guy/gal and one day (this special
thing happens). But because of this guy's/gal's problem (pathology/
character deficit), he/she now finds him-/herself (where?).

THE CHARACTER

Because you are writing about a single main character, give him/her
a name (remember, this is like your child. Treat him/her like a living
thing!). Think about why you are putting your character through
this story. When you come up with that, you will have . . .

THE VALUE

This guy/gal needs to go through this ordeal in order to understand . . . (What?)

If you know the ordeal, you are fairly certain about . . .

- The path to satisfaction
- The lesson

THE WORLD AND THE JOURNEY

Now: Through what world will you take your protagonist? In *The
Godfather* it is simply the world of Michael Corleone's family, the
crime family and his normal family. In *Three Days of the Condor* it is
the same city that Joe Turner has always lived in, but now it's fraught
with danger and paranoia. He's a marked man. In *The Hangover* it's
the world of Las Vegas. But not the fun and gambling we all know.
Rather, the broken tilted world that our Three Buddies have left in
their wake from the night before.

THE LOGLINE

So now you can put this into an elegant little statement. This will be
your *logline.* This will embody two important aspects of your story:

- Emotional value
- Story energy

Don't be surprised if it goes through a few changes before you're
done with your first draft. That's because as you launch yourself into
this new project, your imagination will begin to create all sorts of
improvements. By the time you're approaching the end of Act II in
your beat sheet, you'll really begin to see this thing for what it is. It's
a thrilling moment. But you can't jump ahead. Without these careful, thoughtful, purposeful steps, you'll lose both story value and
story energy.

From this simple statement you'll move on to your action

structure statement (see Chapter Two). This will help you crystallize your three acts, the major action chunks and story arcs, and the climax and resolution. Now you're ready to tell the story.

Step by Step by Step by Step by Step by Step: Your Beat Sheet

This is the most important part of your work. Many people ask me, "What's the point?" While many people just want to launch into formatted "pages," without this essential document you will be stalled by page 12. I'm not much of a mind reader, but I have a feeling that you might be part of that group who simply starts writing in format and then expects the wave of your brilliance to carry you through to the end of the script. If you are lucky to be a screenwriting savant, then you really shouldn't have read this far. You probably don't need this book.

But if you're like most of us mortals, the struggle to tell the clearest, most meaningful, most dramatic, and most energy-giving script is to be crazy and passionate with your beat sheet.

This is sometimes also called the "story outline" or "step outline" or "scene outline" or "step sheet." All virtually the same thing. I like "beat sheet" because it sounds good.

The nickname for this document has several sources. Many say it's because it represents the rhythmic units of your story. Like musical notes, you are putting in metric beats to complete a fully rhythmic story.

In fact, the word *beat* comes from a misnomer; a verbal error on both the part of the speaker and the listener.

Way back in the 1930s there was a very brilliant fellow named Richard Boleslavsky, a Polish film and stage director who had studied the great acting technique of the time, "The Method," from the source itself, Constantin Stanislavski at the Moscow Arts Theater.

He came to New York in the early 1930s where he taught acting to the three greatest acting teachers of the twentieth century, Lee Strasberg, Stella Adler, and Harold Clurman.

While these three and many other young actors and directors (such as Elia Kazan) were training with Boleslavsky, he would often tell them to stop and " . . . go back to that last beat" in their scene work. These young acolytes were fascinated with this idea. How great that dramatic action could be distilled into a metric like musical beats.

But in fact, they were mishearing the brilliant teacher. Because of his thick Russian accent, the word he was actually saying, *bit*, came out as "beet" and so the acting "beat" was born. Since then we have always used this term to describe and track the contiguous segments of dramatic action in a script.

The reason I am asking that you embrace this method is that if you write formatted pages you will easily be able to avoid telling the story. It's so thrilling to write a script! You can describe setting, shots, clothing, and movements; write dialogue and generally get yourself very excited. You look at the page and it's the movie!

But you're not telling the story.

In a beat sheet you cannot avoid telling the story. This is because you are going to describe only the most important and necessary elements of your story. Each beat is roughly equivalent to a scene and location. Sometimes you'll find yourself writing in sequences. But primarily you will be writing — in prose — the "doable" and "sayable" elements of your movie. Here is an example of a beat sheet I created for *Maria Full of Grace*. Please note: this is a beat sheet created after a film has been completely done. You will not find this clarity in your beat sheet until you've been through several drafts.

1. In the night just before dawn, a bus in a small country town in Colombia transports Maria, 17, pretty and brooding, with dozens of other unhappy workers on their daily commute.

2. Rose Factory. It's a mundane, repetitive, impersonal assembly line. Hundreds of workers. Nobody smiles or talks.

Maria pricks her finger on a rose thorn. The only man is the boss who shouts orders to the girls across the vast factory floor.

3. At lunch Maria and her girlfriend Blanca eat at a big lunch-room — a duplicate of the factory. They "check out" another guy at a nearby table who Blanca says has been "looking at her." This is the high point of Blanca's day. Blanca is Maria's best friend and confidante; an ally and protégé.

4. Maria and her boyfriend, Juan, kiss passionately near a deserted building in a quiet, rundown part of town. But Maria is distracted, looking away and up at the roof. She says she has "something to tell him." Juan wants to go to her house to have sex. Maria suggests "up there" on the roof. Juan thinks she's crazy, but she insists. She climbs up on her own, dragging herself up the rough brick wall. She calls Juan up but he won't follow and walks away, leaving her on the roof.

5. At Maria's home her sister struggles with her baby's con-stipation. Maria is critical of her sister's concern. Their grandma sets dinner and suggests a tea for Diana's baby. Maria says, "Those teas don't do anything." The baby cries and Maria insists he's fine. Maria's finicky about dinner. Maria is critical of everyone in her family. More isolation, forcing her toward choices outside of this life.

. . . and so forth. All of your action and dialogue is summarized here. Imagine now how easy it will be to write a screenplay from this material. It's already laid out and there's your story!

By the way, I'm not saying that you should not write pages and scenes. You really should write pages and scenes as your impulses demand. But put them aside for now. Scribble them out, and then put them on the shelf for use later on. Ultimately, they will be used as per the demands of your carefully crafted beat sheet.

Now the only step is to write the script.

Methods to the Madness

How do *you* write? What do you ask of yourself as a writer and artist? I don't know. You have to make that decision. I strongly recommend that you come up with a well-defined schedule. But don't make it difficult. Writing is hard enough, so don't make it any harder than it has to be. If you have other life obligations, you'll need to exercise some sanity.

Do you want to write every day? Okay, then make a schedule you can stick to. The most dispiriting thing is missing your writing schedule. If you're making a commitment, nothing hurts more than when you fail a commitment to yourself. So be sensible. If you can only write one hour per week, then do that. But make it the best hour of writing you can. For myself, because I teach and I'm working on several projects at once, like plays, movies, and books, I schedule things in stretches or in a checkerboard pattern: Script in the morning; book in the afternoon. If my teaching schedule is Tuesday and Friday, then I know I have five days to fit in my writing. But what about laundry, shopping, personal business, my love life? So you fit it in, right? Use your date calendar and really make it a part of your weekly work schedule.

I try to fulfill a certain amount of work each session. If I am creating a beat sheet, I try to do a few beats per day or maybe a full sequence. If I am writing my script pages, then I try to do a good first-draft scene every day. Sometimes I get hot and if I'm working on a multi-scene sequence, I might be able get through it in one session.

I find I can only write from four to six hours per day. It's hard work mentally. If I've got my face in the screen for even an hour, I find I need to come up for air, pace around my apartment, look out the window, or even take a lunch break. But the idea is: "This is what I'm doing with this time *right now*. I'm working!"

This is the mentality you need. So if a friend calls up and says, "Let's hang out," the answer is "No, I'm working." This brings dignity, legitimacy, and self-respect to what you're doing. You don't have to earn money at it for it to be real. You simply have to treat it with respect.

I always lay out deadlines for myself. This means that by a certain date I need to be at a certain point. First, look at your capacity. I believe it takes no less than nine months to complete a spec screenplay from the time you get the idea to the minute you put out the last page of the first draft. Maybe you're quicker or maybe you're slower. But I have rarely completed work of any quality in less time. This book was being outlined five years ago. Then when I got my publisher and an agreement, I had roughly six months to complete what you're reading. This is an "outside" deadline, meaning it's for a buyer, client, or partner.

Your "inside" deadline could vary. That's because you can luxuriate in your writing experience without the bedevilment of a buyer. They can mess with your head sometimes. But if you're working for yourself, you can also be a very bad boss, as in too easy on yourself. So it's important to set deadlines in advance.

Pick a date when you really want to be able to show your first draft. Now back that up two months. That would be the day you want to start writing, which is the day you'll want to have a completed beat sheet. Now back that up about four months. Now back that up a month, and that should be today — the day you thought up your idea and are ready to get started.

Once I have stepped into my script writing, I use a "three window" method when I'm creating script.

Computers are amazing machines for creating stories and scripts. I can gleefully admit that without computers and random access to material, I probably would not be a writer today. I revel in the wonder of this devilish machine, with all its petty annoyances. It's still a miracle of technology.

- In one window I have a single document, which contains my notes, research, and action structure. This window is reserved for all the random ideas, scenes, fragments, and wish lists for your story. This is where you've placed your random scripted scenes. It's also where you can review how this whole thing started.
- In another window, the completed beat sheet.
- In the third and main window, the script, progressing to a first draft.

Tip

I create my beat sheet using my script formatting program rather than a text document. I prefer Movie Magic Screenwriter. Although I write my beats in prose ("action" element), using the screenplay program allows me to see and work with the story and scene structure before I actually write my dialogue and script. I start putting in scene headings and use the navigator panel feature to shift scenes around if necessary. This is also handy if you like to use the index card feature of your program. In this way you're already working with the scene structure of the story before writing the actual screenplay. You also have the flexibility of continuing to develop a strong scene progression before you start writing script pages. Once you're ready to start scripting, you're already in the document.

This way you can now access everything you've ever thought of in your script. However, I caution you. You can go "window blind" if you don't watch out. Screenwriting actually takes a level of clerical organization that is equal to that of some of the best executive office managers or professional assistants. You really need to come up with your own level of organization. It's discouraging to not know where your stuff is.

Maybe you're not a very neat person. I have a very messy desk and if you walked into my home, you'd see any number of things that don't belong where they should. But when it comes to my writing projects, I like to be as organized as a UPS shipping center. I have special names for special documents; folders that have particular functions and time relevance, and a slowly reducing number of documents in my progressive folders. I keep research and notes separate. I name folders "1st Draft," "2nd Draft" and so on. A screenplay is a large, full-length project and you really want to be able to put your hands on something when you need it.

By the way, I know I'm getting close to a finished script when my "scrap" document is about three times longer than my proposed script, around three hundred pages.

Page Count and Structure

Students are always asking me "How many pages in Act I?" And I always very annoyingly answer with a question: "How long is your script?"

I'm not simply being annoying. If you can see the pattern of any story, you can easily see that page count is proportional to the full length of the story. This is proven out in Aristotle by the "golden section" or "golden rectangle."

So here's my quick guide to screenplay beats and page counts (x = a single unit of proportion):

> *Act I:* 10–15 beats; 18–30 pages. Proportion = 1x
> *Act II:* 28–33 beats; 65–80 pages. Proportion = 2½x
> *Act III:* 3–7 beats; 5–20 pages. Proportion = ½x

This all depends on the overall length of your script. But all stories should reflect the same proportions.

As far as page count, don't let it stop you from writing. But you will need to go back and do the most important part of your writing: rewriting.

Any screenwriter will tell you: "Screenwriting is rewriting." This is not simply about your receptivity and flexibility when it comes to notes and criticism. It is the professional mission of any screenwriter to be eager to rewrite. Don't confuse rewriting with "editing," as in deleting or trimming or shortening your prose. Rewriting is the act of perfecting your work of art. It is the only way you will arrive at the completely crystallized story based on your ideas and values. Rewriting means one of the scenes you wrote doesn't work. Paul Attanasio claims to have done nine drafts of the famous "Cake Scene" in *Quiz Show* with Ralph Fiennes and Paul Scofield. Director Robert Redford just kept sending him back until he got it right. And remember, this was a sold script; a done deal. They were going into production. You can bet Attanasio had already done a handful of drafts.

You have to be personally critical when you look at your first draft. Sure, you can revel in being "finished." But you're not. You're at the beginning of a new process, the first part of which is your own critical eye on your work.

When I'm done with an un-commissioned ("spec") first draft (meaning I don't have a partner or a buyer yet) I let it sit there for about two weeks. Then I go in and read, usually aloud from the top. I try to be viscerally alert to what's wrong with it. I try to be merciless with what I've done. I'm never as merciless as some colleagues. This does not mean "nasty" or "destructive," it just means you're ready to cut the fat from your story. If you're showing it to the right people (see Chapter 9) then you'll get the feedback you need and deserve. But you must be ready to shake your head at something you've spent months writing and say, "It doesn't work" or "It's gotta go" or "What was I thinking?" As the great novelist William Faulkner famously said, "You must kill your little darlings" and no more an accurate statement about rewriting has ever been made.

Writing = Writing, So Write!

The very act of writing produces writing. So even if you're stuck on a story problem or, worst of all, you're not writing, simply sit down at the keyboard and just write it out. I guarantee that you'll find something that you need and you can use in your story or in resolving your problem. But watch out that you've laid out all the proper groundwork. As Billy Wilder said, "If you've got a problem in your third act, it's because you got a problem in your first act!" Sometimes the solution to your problem is that you haven't been thoughtful enough. Here are some questions to always ask yourself at every point in your writing:

- Have I created a story of real value? Are the stakes high enough to create distress for the character and audience?
- Is there conflict in every moment of this story? Am I being too easy on the character?
- Does everything connect and fit together in a progression of rising anxiety?
- Is my climax the worst that the main character can imagine — and also the best thing that can happen in my story?
- Is what I'm doing serving the story?
- Is your character's bad fortune, your audience's good fortune?

You're Married to Your Story Now — So Be Faithful!

Which brings me to a very important concept. It's fun to think up your idea. It's actually fun to discover for yourself that it's a solid idea (the action structure). You can sit back and say, "Hey, this will work!" When you sit down to write your beat sheet for Act I, you'll still be excited: "Hey — this is a real movie!" But then . . .

It's like the dating period in a relationship or the honeymoon period in a marriage. After a while — it's work. Now you have to settle down and live with this thing. Part of that is being faithful.

You can't just run around with every idea in town. You can't suddenly switch from a romantic comedy to a film noir. You can't just put a murder mystery in your political drama because it "feels good." I'm asking that you show discipline and commitment to your story and your main character. Use every ounce of self-restraint to keep your story on track. This means always asking the above questions. I assure you that if you sufficiently integrate the values of your story and if you are assured of the importance of the outcome, you won't have a problem.

When the moment comes and you ask, "Who am I writing this script for?" the answer must be "I am writing this script for the main character." You're writing it for your guy or gal and you're writing it to show him/her that he/she has to find a new way of dealing with old problems. But who's the hero for your hero?

YOU.

Chapter 9:
....

NOW WHAT?

"Industry Experts": Nine Out of Ten Times — They're Wrong!

A movie's success or failure is based on so many different factors, you would need a very expensive and exotic team of specialists to even come close to any sort of prediction of how it will fare.

Consider this: in the near future, the movie studios and networks have created an online system of distributing unproduced screenplays to the public. Like a billion-person focus group, everyone gets to vote on the quality of the script. This way the risk of making a money-losing picture would be significantly reduced, right? RIGHT?

Of course there is no such system. But why does it sound so absurd?

One reason might be an accepted piece of wisdom: even people who have been reading screenplays for years know that there are so many variables that determine a movie's success. A script might be great, but what if you don't get good enough or big enough stars? What if you get a great director, but a terrible script? And why would anyone want to do a terrible script? Does anybody know?

Because no matter how many years and how many pictures and how much experience, nobody has yet been able to correctly predict a movie's success or failure even half the time. It's an impossible task. And when you sit down with all the research in the world in an attempt to please the largest audience, it still doesn't matter. Suddenly, there's a movie that nobody thought would be a hit and it's raking it in.

So let's agree, there's no way for anyone to say "This will be a success" simply from reading the script. But (big but) many industry professionals know what they like and another even smaller group can tell if a script has this magic integrity we've been talking about. Some people really do know if a script works.

Here's the tough part. Those people who think they know are sometimes only fearful of making a mistake. This includes agents, managers, development people, and studio and network executives. Many of them are mortally afraid of saying "yes" to the wrong thing. When you have doubt, it's just that much easier to say "no." If you have doubts about whether a star will do it or doubts about the budget and the audience or any doubts at all, it's always safer to say "no." Sure you could say "no" to the next big hit. But at least it didn't really cost anyone any money.

These are the types of people you will encounter when you try to sell your script or get a project going. Their decisions are largely governed by fear and self-interest. So you will need to develop a system that will allow your professional life to flourish even in the face of what appears to be this monolithic wall of negativity.

First of all, thick skin does not mean you become a kind of screenwriter-slash-gladiator. But it does mean that when the criticism comes, especially from those who you feel are utterly underqualified, you've got to suck it up, bite that lower lip, and turn into one of those dolls on the rear shelf of a car, and just nod your head. You've also got to learn to listen to and take notes. This is what's expected of you for the value of your paycheck. This doesn't mean the buyer is always right. Creative executives are interested in making the best possible picture they can. But everyone has his/her own concept of a story, so you have to listen and you have to take it seriously.

The second thing you'll have to put up with is the harshly dismissive atmosphere of film and television. Every agent will tell you, "I don't think this picture can be made. You've really missed the mark." Remember: that's just one opinion. *Titanic* was turned down by each studio successively over a four- or five-year period. Then . . . ?

Your job now is to show this script to a trusted few, even if they are not professionals. If you know any actors, that's great, they are a terrific first stop. If you know other filmmakers, pick one or two and use them as a sounding board. The main thing is not to show it to everybody. All you want to do is get a nice cross-section of opinion. I also understand how sensitive and delicate you're going to be about it. I am too. Every screenwriter is. We work our asses off and after someone reads your script all you'll hear is "Interesting." It can drive you nuts.

Then you might be in a situation where you're getting ideas and notes from too many people and thinking that you have to take every single note. It's confusing, but you're permitted to be picky. You will have to determine who comes closest to giving you that great idea or spotting something you really believe will change your script for the better. Remember: you're not there to please the person reading your script. You're there to please the story. It's a tough thing to believe in, but you have the right to stick to your guns.

If you're in a production or preproduction situation, you'll have a handful of people breathing down your neck. If you've been fortunate enough to continue with the project beyond the point of purchase, this means that those in charge are smart enough to stick with a good thing: the original writer. But there's the studio producer and there's the three executive producers from the other production company and there's the star and there's the director. Who are you supposed to listen to?

The rule of thumb would be the person who really has his/her hands on the making of the picture. The default choice in this situation would be the director. However, in many cases, the actual

creative force behind the project may be one of the executive producers. Whatever the case, you'll need to discern the one person who is
really making the picture; the "force" behind it as it were. But you
will also have to show respect for everyone's opinion. If their notes
don't get used because the director won't use them, they can bring
their idea to the director. Sometimes you simply have to say "yes"
because people deserve it once in a while. And even the most annoying collaborator may very well come up with at least one terrific idea.

Whoever you show your script to, you want to pick people who
will respect your efforts, but also give you an honest opinion. One
word of advice: when conferring with anybody and listening to their
notes and questions try to remain calm and silent. Just jot down
their notes. If you get into discussions, especially if you find yourself defending something in your work, watch out. You'll be inhibiting this person. Just be polite and nod. Treat the person like a state
trooper who's pulled you over even though you know you weren't
speeding.

Notes and review are an interesting process. I have been fortunate enough to be part of a writers group in New York for over twenty
years. I've learned to write there and I've become a better writer
because of it. But what I've learned about notes is that any question
is the same as a criticism. That is to say, that if even one listener/
reader has a single question regarding story clarity, meaning, or plot,
then you have to go back in and give it a look. Then see if this issue
was raised by anyone else. If it was, then you have a problem. There's
a very handy expression I use:

> "If twelve Russians tell you you're drunk . . .
> you better lie down."

The goal is to put together a group of friends who can be candid
without being discouraging, who also have decent movie instincts.
Some of these folks can be knowledgeable about films. But they don't

all have to be movie experts. If you can assemble a trusted group of colleagues who can be helpful, then you will have created a support group that can counteract the surreal fears of the industry at large. If you feel your script works and then you get this reinforced, you can go out into the world with the confidence you'll need to keep going. Many professional screenwriters and screenwriting teachers have their own websites. John August's site is something I look at occasionally because he is so smart and because I admire his work so much. There are hundreds of sites to choose from with lots of useful advice. Notice I'm pointing you toward screenwriters. These are the best people I know and I revel in the attentions of a fellow or sister writer. They really know what's what.

There are also a lot of script and story consultants like myself. My site is www.StoryRescue.com. I've coached and consulted with dozens of screenwriters, playwrights, TV writers, and novelists about their stories. It's all a matter of what you're looking for and that "fit." Listen to the person who makes the most sense.

Some of the fees can be high, but some are suspiciously low (you get what you pay for!). Just be sensible. How much can you afford? How much are you getting for your money? Like myself, almost all of these consultants will chat or email with you to give you a better idea of their services.

It's Your Script and You'll Write What You Want To!

John August, the brilliant screenwriter of *Big Fish* and *Charlie and the Chocolate Factory*, once said in an interview (I paraphrase), "When you're trying to make it as a screenwriter, there are these tall, thick stone walls you have to break through. You keep pounding and scraping away and then you finally break through this almost impenetrable wall, and there, on the other side, is another huge stone wall." Heard this before? "Sorry, they're only looking for . . . rom-coms/slasher pics/horror adventures/historical drama/gay coming of age — or was it sci-fi?"

You'll get onto the web and find one of those sites that claims to be at the cutting edge of movies and TV; the clearinghouse for everything that's "saleable." And then you'll be the victim of the worst thing possible: trend. That's right. The "Flavor of the Month," the "Newest Thing." Now everyone wants to see teen vampire scripts and the next week it's neo-noir and pretty soon your head is spinning off your shoulders.

Don't fall into the trap. Be true to the script you are writing.

Sure you have to know your genre, but *don't try to write the script that everybody will like.* You can't do it and it doesn't exist.

The only script you have the authority to write is the script you really see clearly in your creative mind. Stick with it. You'll be constantly discouraged. But if you work hard enough and with enough honesty, you'll write the script that really shows your creative abilities, not somebody else's and not "the herd's."

The idea in this business is to stand out, not to blend in. You won't get any attention otherwise. The list is long of screenwriters who tried to please the crowd only to learn that the script that was in their hearts was the one that would bring them success. The old adage "Be true to yourself" is very applicable here. That doesn't mean you become a stubborn or unreasonable professional. But it does mean you write what you believe will work and then reasonably tailor it to the market, provided that you have a market. Just don't go crazy trying to second-guess everything. You'll never win.

The Three Ds

DILIGENT: Pick a project. Make a deadline. Finish it.

DEVOTED: You're an artist. Get the professional training you think you need. You have a vision. Be part of the community. See movies. Read scripts. Learn about the colleagues in your profession and be part of it.

DETERMINED: Be fearless. Be professional. When you've

reached a milestone in your work, show it to somebody. When you're done, get it out there.

"A good story is a miracle." —Stanley Kubrick

This was Kubrick's benediction on the moment of finding a story that works. He made only twelve movies in his career. If anything, he was picky. But he also recognized that you can't just go out there and find or make a good story. There are so many variables that go into the creation of a script, not to mention a finished movie, that the whole process seemed miraculous to him. It still is for most of us, regardless of our long experience.

The miracle comes from the fact that as artists we have the distinct privilege to create something from nothing. Nobody else really has that opportunity, except for those who are colonists of some remote, unoccupied land. So the first miracle is that you're an artist.

The second miracle is that you have vision. You have an idea. You want to tell a story. You can sit down and write it. Then you can share it with the world. You have created a document that has meaning and can be performed. Wow.

The third miracle (because you have to have threes!) is that you have the necessary skills and talent to do it. This means you've studied your craft. It means you've opened your mind to the knowledge you'll need to be a professional.

You can't just sit down and do this. You have to know what you're doing.

"Copying" Is Plagiarism. "Stealing" Is Art!

I'm a big fan of knowing a lot. Because I specialize in fact-based stories, every time I sit down to write a new project, I learn about a whole new world. I'm now an expert on ham radio. I also wrote a script about a global gold mining scandal in Indonesia. I'm an expert on all that now. And one of my plays is about football concussions, so now I know all about football and neuroscience, two topics I never knew much about.

This is a way of saying you have to be open to the mere adventure of writing. You also have to be open to everything that has come before. You must be an expert on films or TV or both. Try to see every movie ever made. With online streaming, TV On Demand, and everything else available to you, you really have no excuse. It's important that you not only watch all the great movies (yes, you can start with the "AFI 100") but you should watch at least every successful movie. This means anything critically successful and/or commercially successful. You have an obligation as a professional to know your art — and I don't mean "arty." If sci-fi is your thing, then certainly see every decent sci-fi movie. But also see everything else. Every movie can give you some insight about how to handle a character or story problem.

Today, with the Internet, you now have the ability to download and read some of the greatest screenplays ever written in their original form. There are a handful of websites with free downloads and a few more where you might pay a few bucks. It's really worth it. To see and analyze the work of professional screenwriters is the best way to get underneath the conceptual and see the practical. How does this writer describe an action sequence? How does another writer deal with dialogue? How many pages can be spent on one scene? All of these questions can be easily answered if you just start to explore the vast amount of information that's out there.

This brings me back to the heading of this section—"'Copying' Is Plagiarism. 'Stealing' is Art." I don't know where I first heard this, but it's one of my main credos. I don't think there's a single completely "original" movie out there, no more than there is a completely "original" human being. What I mean is that we've all got the same organs. We all function in almost identical ways, yet we're all remarkably different.

Same with movies. They are all made up of primarily the same parts, but combined in uniquely different ways. So no matter where you steal your ideas from (and I encourage you to do it in an artful and ingenious way) you will make them your own. It's inevitable. Your DNA, your personality will allow you to make something original no matter what you do. So be mindful when the muse is talking to you. Write everything down, then sit at your work space on a very regular basis and make something!

Get It Out There!

So the time has come. You've finished a draft. You know who you're going to go to for advice and good, supportive notes. You're going to listen and then you're going to spend some time rewriting. You'll feel like this has taken forever, but maybe it's only been six months or maybe two years. It doesn't matter how fast you can do it, it only matters how you stuck with it and how you finished.

There are numbers of ways of "getting it out there." Of course we all want to strike it rich, so everyone thinks if you get a network or a studio to look at your work, everything will be fine. I hate to break the news, but you'll need an agent. And getting an agent can seem as impossible as winning the lottery. Most agents have their hands full with enough clients, only a small percentage of whom are earning any money. Agents can only legally claim 10% of those earnings, so they'll need quite a few clients to make a dollar for themselves. So here comes you, an untried, unproduced, new screenwriter and the last thing they need. Fundamentally they can't tell if your script is any good. They'll need to hear that from someone else.

So here's where you need to be clever and tenacious. I always advise the "home-grown" method. If you can get your script produced locally, that's the best way to go. If you can direct it, even better. Raise a few hundred thousand bucks and make your movie. Sounds easy, but of course it's not. But you'll expend the same time, energy, and heartache trying to get industry people to read your script and in the end, you won't have a movie. You make the choice.

Another way to do it is script contests, festivals, and grants. Look them over. See which ones make the most sense to you. Of course, the most prestigious such as the Sloan Foundation, Sundance Workshop, and the Nichols Fellowship are very competitive. But it's a competitive business. Get into the fray and see what happens.

You're not only putting your script out there, but you're also putting yourself out there. It's scary, I know. But if you don't take these kinds of risks, where would you be? Like a main character who's going to change, you need to be going somewhere and for a very good reason.

So go. Write. DO IT!

APPENDIX

RECOMMENDED VIEWING (. . . and spoiler alert)

The following films are referred to in detail in this book. It is highly recommended that you view these films. Of course if you haven't tried to see every movie ever made, start today. It's part of your job as a screenwriter.

If you haven't seen these films, the book spares no details in revealing their plots and endings, surprise and otherwise.

Indicates repeated reference and used as prime examples. These are especially important to see.

*Adaptation

*Bicycle Thieves (or "The Bicycle Thief")

*Casablanca

*Chinatown

*Courage Under Fire

*Dr. Strangelove . . .

*The Road to El Dorado

*Following

*Get Him to the Greek

*Heat

*Hot Tub Time Machine

*Jaws

*Looper

*Maria Full of Grace

*Memento

*Midnight Cowboy

*Paper Moon

*Quiz Show

*Run Lola Run

*Silver Linings Playbook

*Star Wars

*The Godfather (I & II)

*The Hangover

*Thief

*Three Days of the Condor

*Up in the Air

12 Years a Slave

9 to 5

A Beautiful Mind

A Day in the Life of An American Fireman

American Hustle

Annie Hall

Apollo 13

Bambi

Barry Lyndon

Big Sleep, The

ACKNOWLEDGMENTS

A brief note of thanks to a few people without whom this book would never have found its way out of my head.

My deepest thanks to DB Gilles whose extraordinary books on this subject are an inspiration to us all. He has been my great friend and colleague at NYU since 1999 and without his encouragement and hand-holding, this would never have been written.

To all my colleagues at NYU's Kanbar Undergraduate Film & TV Department, most notably Paul Thompson, who all continue to teach me to be a better teacher.

Thanks to my colleagues at Hollins University. To Tim Albaugh for his leadership and acumen and who keeps me hot for Hollywood. He introduced me to the master himself, Hal Ackerman whose imprint upon this craft has proven indelible. His books and lectures inspire me.

Much thanks to Gary Sunshine, my extraordinary copy editor who really read this right and tenderly told me how to make it better.

And finally, to my students everywhere who bless me with their curiosity and their struggle to make a story work. They continue to remind me how much we all love it. I thank them for humbling me and teaching me how much I still need to learn.

Many thanks,
Joe Gilford
Brooklyn, NY
December, 2014

ABOUT THE AUTHOR

Eric Etheridge

JOE GILFORD is a thirty-five-year veteran writer, director, and producer. His upcoming feature screenplays, *Kalimantan* and *Moonbounce*, are currently in preparation. He has written documentaries for PBS' award-winning *American Experience*. He has been one of the most popular professors at NYU's undergraduate film department since 1999. He teaches and lectures nationwide and has also been on the faculty at Columbia University, Montclair State University, and Hollins University in Virginia. He is an in-demand script consultant through his website StoryRescue.com, consulting with dozens of writers on their screenplays, TV scripts, plays, and novels. He is the recipient of an Alfred P. Sloan Foundation grant for his play *Danny's Brain* about football concussions. His off-Broadway play *Finks* was critically acclaimed and nominated for two Drama Desk Awards, including Outstanding Play and an Off-Broadway Alliance award for Best New Play. The play was videotaped for the prestigious Lincoln Center Theater on Film collection, usually reserved for Broadway productions. *Finks* is published by Dramatists Play Service.

How to contact Joe Gilford: www.StoryRescue.com or info@storyrescue.com

See more about Joe Gilford and his work at: www.JoeGilford.com

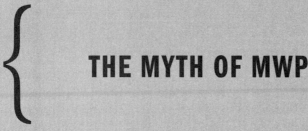

THE MYTH OF MWP

In a dark time, a light bringer came along, leading the curious and the frustrated to clarity and empowerment. It took the well-guarded secrets out of the hands of the few and made them available to all. It spread a spirit of openness and creative freedom, and built a storehouse of knowledge dedicated to the betterment of the arts.

The essence of the Michael Wiese Productions (MWP) is empowering people who have the burning desire to express themselves creatively. We help them realize their dreams by putting the tools in their hands. We demystify the sometimes secretive worlds of screenwriting, directing, acting, producing, film financing, and other media crafts.

By doing so, we hope to bring forth a realization of 'conscious media' which we define as being positively charged, emphasizing hope and affirming positive values like trust, cooperation, self-empowerment, freedom, and love. Grounded in the deep roots of myth, it aims to be healing both for those who make the art and those who encounter it. It hopes to be transformative for people, opening doors to new possibilities and pulling back veils to reveal hidden worlds.

MWP has built a storehouse of knowledge unequaled in the world, for no other publisher has so many titles on the media arts. Please visit www.mwp.com where you will find many free resources and a 25% discount on our books. Sign up and become part of the wider creative community!

Onward and upward,

Michael Wiese
Publisher/Filmmaker